I0093277

"Bold and counterintuitive. *Redundant Charities* will make you rethink the business of giving and have you questioning whose interests are really served. An important read for anyone who cares about inequality"

Antoinette Lattouf

Broadcaster, columnist and author of *How to Lose Friends and Influence White People*

"In *Redundant Charities*, Weh Yeoh makes a convincing case for the virtues of obsolescence: that the goal of any non-profit should be to make itself unnecessary. In this wry and incisive book, Yeoh offers a much-needed antidote to the corporate thinking and big-is-better mentality that have come to plague the non-profit industrial complex, to the detriment of donors and recipients alike. He then shows how charity work could be better: more self-aware, more far-sighted, and ultimately more effective. Anyone who works for a non-profit, or aspires to, should read this book."

Sebastian Strangio

Author of *Cambodia: From Pol Pot to Hun Sen and Beyond*

REDUNDANT CHARITIES

escaping the cycle of dependence

WEH YEOH

First published in Australia 2023
Published by Koan Press
redundantcharities.com

Photographs supplied.

ISBN: 978-0-6457280-0-2

NATIONAL LIBRARY OF AUSTRALIA

A catalogue record for this
work is available from the
National Library of Australia

Book design: WorkingType Studio

Contents

Foreword   I

Part 1:   **The Old Model Is Broken**   11

Chapter 1   *The growth obsession*   13

Chapter 2   *The self obsession*   21

Chapter 3   *The hamster wheel*   34

Chapter 4   *When there's no end point*   49

Part 2:   **How to Set Up a Redundant Charity**   61

Chapter 5   *Defining an end point*   63

Chapter 6   *Defining an exit strategy*   77

Chapter 7   *Executing an exit strategy*   94

Part 3:   **Your Role in Redundant Charities**   113

Chapter 8.   *Taking steps towards redundancy*   115

Conclusion   121

Acknowledgements   125

References   127

Foreword

I was never a good student. I'd studied physiotherapy because I knew I didn't have what it took to become a doctor — I'd seen my eldest brother go through that — and yet I wanted to do something vaguely health related. I loved playing sports. That was a good start, wasn't it?

I grew up in Sydney. I'd had the privilege of going to a private school. All in all, I'd lived a really sheltered life. As often happens, I didn't have dreams of my own, I only had other people's.

That's why every semester at university would follow a familiar pattern. I'd turn up to lectures bleary-eyed after yet another late night for the most part, and then rote learn as much as possible before the end-of-semester exams.

My heart wasn't in it. I can't even recall many of the things I learnt at the time.

My entire physiotherapy career lasted two years. It was an out-and-out failure.

Strangely though, I do remember one important detail. It began a lifelong interrogation into the effectiveness of charities. It would lead me to volunteering in a small Vietnamese community with vulnerable children. I would work for both a small and a large charity, neither of which seemed ideal. For someone highly critical of charities, I would make the most illogical decision — I would start my own. And I would take to the TEDx stage to share my understanding of how charities can be more effective.

All of this started from one seemingly unrelated lecture on ethics in physiotherapy. It was 2001. I was sitting in the Cumberland Campus of Sydney University.

Here's what I learnt:

Helen, a 46-year-old accountant, visits her local physiotherapist, Madhuri, after injuring her back playing tennis on the weekend. Initially, Helen is paying Madhuri for sympathy as much as she is for treatment. After all, she's in pain, and she expects Madhuri to not only hear her out but also give her a massage. There's definitely something healing about human touch when you're in pain.

Madhuri has a choice. She can acquiesce to Helen's expectations by applying treatment like ice, heat or massage. If she does so, she'll keep Helen coming back to the clinic as long as these treatments reduce Helen's pain.

But Madhuri knows that an ethical physiotherapist would help Helen become independent. She could give her exercises or education. Helen could then implement these exercises in her own time, either in the office or at home, to fix the underlying issue causing her back pain.

This is the difference between addressing symptoms and solving the underlying problem. An ethical physiotherapist breaks the business model. That's the point. A truly successful physiotherapist is one who isn't needed anymore.

It takes a level of integrity and self-sacrifice to achieve the outcomes needed for your patient. You have to take your ego and your bank account out of it. It has to be about something bigger than yourself.

It strikes me that many charities could learn from this approach.

Imagine if charities looked to solve underlying problems instead of addressing symptoms. Imagine if charities looked to break their own business model. We would have to redefine what a successful charity is. We would focus less on the charity and what it's achieving now, and more on the legacy it leaves behind.

This would be a shift in thinking from the here and now, from the short term to the long term. This shift would require a level of integrity that I rarely saw in my brief career working with charities.

I want to make something very clear. It would be easy to blame people who work within charities for the state of the charity sector. But I believe that almost everyone who works within a charity has the best of intentions. And there are plenty of examples worldwide of charities who are doing incredible work and changing the world for the better.

In order to propose a new model of charities, it's necessary for me to showcase some of the worst of charities and show why their design often prevents them from making themselves redundant. The key word to highlight in that sentence is *design*. Charities are the way they are, not because people who start charities or work within them are bad but because the structure of charities is inherently flawed. This is one of the reasons why charities so often go wrong. But to change an entire sector we first need to change our perspectives. Few stories illustrate this more than this one.

In India, people from a Western charity noticed a group of women carrying water in drums balanced on their heads from the river to the village — a 14-kilometre round trip. The foreigners saw this as a huge waste of time and so, with the approval of the village elders, built a well in the centre of the town square.

When they came back a year later, they noticed to their dismay that no one was using the well. It wasn't broken, and it wasn't that the villagers didn't know how to use or maintain it.

What could possibly have gone wrong?

I often tell this story when I teach university students the principles of redundant charities. In asking hundreds of students this question, very rarely does anyone come to the answer immediately.

When asked why they didn't use the well, the women of the village told the foreigners: "No one asked us whether or not we needed the well. You see us walking to the river to gather water as a waste of time. We don't. We see it as an opportunity to talk about how useless the men in the village are."

What this story illustrates so well is how much our own thinking, biases and lived experiences cloud our judgement. If you come from a Western country, it is easy to empathise with the foreign charity workers, armed with productivity apps and their own views on efficiency. It's almost impossible to do good without being influenced by the self.

The charity thought that it could help solve a problem for the women villagers, but in reality it was only ever addressing a symptom, albeit ineffectively. From the charity's point of view, it's much easier and much quicker to just address symptoms.

This approach is even more tempting when the average charity worker is equipped with multiple university degrees. With so much training under your belt, it's tempting to think that you don't have to consult or learn anything new.

Solving underlying problems, on the other hand, involves much more work. For starters, it involves challenging our own concepts and beliefs.

This involves a complete rethink of what a successful charity looks like. It's a significant mindset shift from the traditional model of charity, which defines success narrowly.

A redundant charity defines success through no longer being needed.

* * *

"It's a good cause."

When you're stopped in the street by a smiling charity worker, when a chocolate-box-wielding colleague appeals for your hard-earned cash or when you hear about somebody volunteering their precious time over the weekend, you'll often hear the above phrase.

As someone who worked in the non-profit sector for more than a decade — and who has founded charities in Australia and Cambodia — there are few things that make me shudder more than hearing, "It's a good cause."

Phrases like "it's a good cause" give blanket endorsement to any venture deemed charitable in nature. It's this attitude that promotes more and more charities being started in the world.

I often wondered how it was possible that countries like Cambodia had literally hundreds of charities, some of which had over 1,000 employees.

They seemed so distant from my understanding of charity. It never made sense to me that charities should boast about how big they are, or how much growth they achieve.

How does this happen? It happens when we give charities a free pass with "it's a good cause."

You're reading a book called *Redundant Charities*. Chances are that while you believe charities play a role in improving society and the planet, you feel the sector has somewhat lost its way.

You probably believe that we shouldn't give blanket support to all causes. You likely believe that some causes receive too much attention compared to others that are equally or more worthy. And you probably believe that just because someone works for or starts a charity, it doesn't mean that their intentions are pure.

If I got those assumptions wrong, I'm not sure if this is the right book for you.

This book is for you if you want to apply a critical lens to any supposedly "good cause"; if you wonder why there are so many charities in the world, many seemingly working towards the same goal; or if you are willing to question why charities feel the need to stick around in various countries, often for decades, delivering largely imperceptible changes in the lives of those they claim to be helping or saving.

So, what is a redundant charity?

A redundant charity is a response to a pattern of charity failures that I had witnessed in my early career.

Prior to starting my first charity in Cambodia in 2013, a charity named OIC Cambodia, I had worked in the non-profit sector and studied international development in Australia for a number of years. Despite being only 32, I had seen my fair share of the worst behaviour that a charity could exhibit.

I'd worked for a small charity and learnt that good intentions were not enough. I'd also worked with a large international charity that seemed more interested in perpetuating its own existence than delivering real value to people.

I'd also co-founded a non-profit, WhyDev, that aimed to answer the question "How do we get development right?". It turns out it wasn't a question easily answered.

All of this led me to Cambodia, where I learnt that there was not one single Cambodian speech therapist in the country. Naively, I decided that I had to start a charity to solve the problem. This charity would work with the government to develop the in-country profession of speech therapy so that the over half a million people needing support there could access it.

When I started OIC Cambodia, I had two principles in mind. Firstly, the charity had to, as soon as possible, be led by a Cambodian person.

I was sick of seeing so many foreigners in Cambodia, helping local people 'build their capacity' while being paid Western wages and living hedonistic lifestyles. Born in Australia to migrant parents from Malaysia, I had heard so much about the impact of colonialism on Asian lives. Although I had no Cambodian heritage, I felt an instant connection to the struggles of Cambodian people as they dealt with the fallout of French colonial rule, and then the impact of well-meaning Westerners forcing their will on the country. It seemed wrong that Westerners felt they could tell Cambodians how to fix their own problems.

The second principle was that the charity had to have a defined ending, and support had to exit the country at that point. It seemed that charities often fell into this trap whereby they focussed heavily on self-perpetuation rather than solving a problem once and for all.

Having an end point where the charity could walk away — this seemed like the only logical solution to the problem.

OIC Cambodia was my first attempt to put into practice the principles outlined in this book. I want to propose and promote a new idea of how to best help: that a successful charity isn't one that dedicates itself indefinitely to a cause in order to justify its own existence in the eyes of stakeholders or contributors. A successful charity, rather, is one that strives consciously to make itself disappear.

As a redundant charity, OIC Cambodia is led by a local team in Cambodia and it's crucial that I'm not too heavily involved. The irony is that it means I am under qualified to talk about how my vision of OIC Cambodia has played out in reality. Therefore, when I speak about OIC Cambodia, I'll be speaking more to the intent behind it, rather than the reality.

However, much like the phrase "it's a good cause", the situation is not black and white. It would be remiss of me to only highlight the negatives and not engage with the grey. In Part 2 of the book, I'll talk through not only how redundancy can be achieved, but also about some charities that are achieving this goal. In Part 3, I'll talk about your role, as the reader of this book, in supporting the principles of redundant charities.

I'll use the phrases non-profit, charity, not-for-profit and NGO interchangeably. Although they all mean different things to different people, I'm using them to represent an organisation that exists to help people or the planet, regardless of the structure. I'll talk a lot about international examples, because it's often easier to observe power dynamics in these settings. Although the Redundant Charity model cannot be applied to each and every charity in the world, I believe these principles can be applied to many charities, domestic or international.

In writing this book, I've relied heavily on my own experiences working in Australia and overseas, but also on interviews with leading charity experts and founders. These are people who are also frustrated with the status quo of charities, and operate all the way along the spectrum of change, from investigating the redundant charity model to having successfully closed down charities.

This book exists to showcase a new model of charity, a model that's not self-serving, a model that delivers outcomes, a model that enables people to be empowered rather than being stripped of their power.

So, let's start reimagining what a charity should be.

Part 1

The Old Model is Broken

.

Chapter 1

The growth obsession

Private sector infiltration of charities

Jane works a 60-hour week at a large accounting firm. Since the onset of a global pandemic, she starts to wonder why she works so hard for her private sector clients. She has three children and, with her partner recently being made redundant from his job, she's concerned that they may not have enough money to continue to send their children to private school.

Her circumstances don't allow for a career change. At the same time, she decides she wants to give back and starts volunteering on the board of a local not-for-profit helping recently settled asylum seekers. With barely enough time as it is to maintain work and life balance, she finds herself increasingly stretched. And yet, she's worked for a top tier firm, and her non-profit colleagues respect what she says. After three years on the board, a former asylum seeker who volunteers with the charity starts to ask questions about the board and how they were selected. It seems that the board is predominantly made up of white, middle-class volunteers who are friends of the founder. Prompted by this conversation, Jane starts to realise that she has not yet met one single asylum seeker.

How many of us know of someone like Jane?

The private sector infiltration of charities has been insidious, and yet, the consequences are significant.

When people like Jane "give back", they take their private sector mindset and apply it to the non-profit sector. One good example is the UK's MSI Reproductive Choices' (formerly Marie Stopes) CEO Simon Cooke, who, in 2019, received a significant bonus, thus boosting his annual salary to £434,000. What was it that prompted the Marie Stopes' board to approve this salary increase?

The charity was able to fundraise £700,000 more that year compared to the last. It seemed reasonable to the board to allocate a significant amount of that income to the man who led the team (Weymouth, 2019). Another way of viewing this justification is that CEOs like Cooke are paid more money to grow a charity, not to shrink it.

Articles in the *Financial Review* provide guides on 'how to make the leap from corporate to not-for-profit', complete with the ear-to-ear grin of Starlight Children's Foundation CEO Louise Baxter, presumably illustrating the joy of such a career move (Boddy, 2020). It's worth noting that there are no guides or articles promoting how a non-profit CEO might make the career move to a corporation.

And it's not just CEOs. Most major companies engage employee-led corporate social responsibility (CSR) committees, who get to distribute significant amounts of resources such as staff time or money. Anecdotally, these committees are filled with well-meaning people with little to no non-profit or community training — essentially whoever is willing to give up their time.

Board members from the private sector are seen to legitimise the otherwise amateur nature of non-profits. This is despite board members from big business overseeing one of the worst scandals in non-profit history. In 1992, the CEO of United Way, one of the biggest charities in the world, based in the United States, misused funds for personal reasons, including courting a 17-year-old sister of a staff member (Shapiro, 2011). This occurred despite a 37-member board and a 14-member executive committee. Only three of the 37-member board came from the non-profit world (Grant, 1992). United Way is an organisation structured with a large number of local chapters, and yet, there was not a single board seat reserved for a local chapter.

At the time, Kenneth L Albrecht, president of the National Charities Information Bureau said: "In the '80s, charities were told to be more businesslike, which is wrong. Business is not the only role model, they don't do everything right" (Grant, 1992).

Corporations like to partner with charities, either through volunteering or fundraising. Unintentionally, this further promotes growth in non-profits, as big corporations prefer to engage like for like. This is because corporations openly admit that partnering with charities is an exercise in increasing staff engagement. I truly believe that management does care about the missions of charities, but equally, charity involvement is an exercise in being seen to do good. Partnering with charities is a branding exercise.

It follows that a Goldman Sachs would much rather proclaim support for an Oxfam or World Vision than a small volunteer-run charity without the same name power.

Bigger non-profits are seen as more trustworthy, with better mechanisms to report on use of funds. Of course, being able to report on the effectiveness of your work is not the same as being able to be effective in your work.

These partnerships enable larger charities, who already have access to more resources, to access even more resources.

The insidious infiltration by the private sector has permanently affected the mindset of the non-profit sector.

Charities think growth is success

One clear way that private sector logic has infiltrated non-profits is through the idea that bigger is better. This is a notion that is rarely challenged.

Non-profits, including those whose very design prevents them from being effective at scale, love to boast about size. "We have headquarters in 25 countries! We have 1,000 staff in Malawi! We raised $108 million last year, up from $78 million the year before!"

Charities will often talk about scale, as if scale alone implies that their work is effective. But none of these boasts say anything about the effectiveness of a charity's work. They tell us about the capacity (country offices and staff size) and the inputs (donation size) but nothing about the outputs (effect on people's lives). Scale does not necessarily equal success.

However, for the survival of the non-profit, bigger clearly is better, particularly when it results in stamping out competition.

Bigger non-profits can attract greater "market share" — the very definition of private sector logic — by out-competing other non-profits for funding. More resources to begin with mean greater resources to lobby and advocate for more funding.

In Australia, half of the revenue in the charity sector goes to the largest 0.4% of charities. Another way of thinking of this is that of

the roughly 48,000 charities registered with the national body —
the Australian Charities and Not-for-profits Commission (ACNC)
— 192 charities consume half of the available income (ACNC, 2021).
With large fundraising teams and greater institutional trust, it
becomes increasingly common for large charities to push smaller
charities out of the way.

---

*"Charities will often talk about scale, as if scale alone
implies that their work is effective."*

This is also common on the world scale. In September 2000,
the United Nations member states signed off on the Millennium
Development Goals — eight ambitious goals to better the world by
2015 (WHO, 2018). Goal 6 was to "Combat HIV/AIDS, malaria and
other diseases", a bold move to call out two specific disease areas that
needed attention. Unfortunately, these two causes diverted funding
away from other needy health efforts (Shiffman, 2008). The creation
of the Global Fund to Fight AIDS, Tuberculosis and Malaria likely
involved some focussed lobbying to shuffle the disease in under the
'other diseases' umbrella, and was pushed by groups who would
benefit from tuberculosis funding (Smith & Taylor, 2013).

A cause that already has more resources can outcompete other
causes, further funnelling resources in its direction.

To be clear, a non-profit that grows is not, in and of itself,
problematic. Logically, scale allows non-profits to reach more people
and do more good. However, when a non-profit focuses on growth,

often at the expense of effectiveness, the mission can easily deviate towards self-perpetuation.

Charities are self-perpetuating

In the north-west of England lies a tiny little town named Luckington. It's unlikely you would have heard of it. In 2006, rising waters in the River Avon made part of a road impossible to cross. Markers were placed on either side to warn drivers not to attempt the cross.

Despite this, one to two cars a day still drove past warning signs and went right into the river for the two weeks following the closure. Why? Drivers were so focussed on their GPS displays, which confidently told them to continue driving, that they didn't notice what was in front of them (Perton, 2022).

Charities are much like these cars, and charity leadership much like the drivers. Their internal plans suggest that growth is the way forward, but the reality of the situation in front of them states otherwise.

It is always assumed that bigger is better in charities. A charity's mission statement — their reason for existing — may well be "To provide clean drinking water to all", but that's not necessarily why it continues to exist. The real mission is to keep the wheels of the charity turning.

It takes a lot of effort to establish a non-profit — years of work and thousands of dollars in legal fees. For non-profits to throw this all away is counterintuitive (Yeoh & Smith, 2021).

In his seminal book, *Thinking, Fast and Slow*, Nobel laureate

Daniel Kahneman describes a psychological bias known as sunk cost fallacy. This occurs when additional resources, including time, are devoted to a particular cause despite minimal gains being observed. For charities, often, so much effort has been invested in a non-profit in the past, that, despite it no longer serving its purpose, people continue to invest more in its future (Bosten, 2021).

If the pathway to doing more good is via scale, the focus of the non-profit becomes about maintaining and growing the enterprise, rather than achieving the mission. After all, there are salaries to pay and lives that depend on those salaries.

"the focus of the non-profit becomes about maintaining and growing the enterprise"

In private conversations, CEOs of large non-profits have expressed their concern over what would happen to their staff if their non-profit were to intentionally shrink. "No one wants to be the CEO of a charity that tells his staff they don't have jobs anymore," I've been told. This is a very common mindset.

It's admirable when CEOs care about the livelihoods of their staff. However, more admirable is drawing a line in the sand and realising that your staff are secondary to the cause.

It reminds me of my dad hanging on to an old piece of technology like a CD player. His children have gifted him a Spotify subscription, and yet, he continues to hang on to the CD player out of loyalty to the CD collection he spent decades curating. Despite the options,

Dad has made a choice to maintain the status quo. So too have charities.

The natural progression of the sunk cost fallacy is to dig your heels in and protect what you have worked so hard to produce. And when threats arise in the form of competition, this leads to non-profits attempting to discredit other non-profits.

When I worked in Cambodia, one of the favourite pastimes of expat charity workers would be to sit in a bar bad mouthing other charities and the work they did: "This particular charity misspent these funds," or "This one caught the CEO embezzling funds and did nothing about it," for example.

These discussions may be mindless fun, but they are also an insight into the mistrust between charities.

As with most workplaces, identity becomes really important. Like fans of a football team, you'll hear staff of certain charities pledge their allegiance through statements like, "I'm an Oxfam guy, not a World Vision guy."

And much like football fans going to a game, charities reinforce this through making their staff wear branded t-shirts when out and about.

Ultimately, it becomes about identity. A strong identity as a charity worker leads to the involvement of ego. It's natural that charity workers would identify as inherently good people.

Chapter 2

The self obsession

When the ego provides motivation

"To be or to do? Which way will you go?"
—John Boyd

My first non-profit role was in China. Sitting on a plane, travelling back from China to Australia after 12 months of working with children with disabilities, I started to think about how I would introduce myself to people I met socially on my return.

"Oh, I'm an aid worker who worked in one of the poorest provinces in China." Or maybe: "I'm a charity worker for kids with disabilities."

None of the statements sat right with me. But then I caught myself wondering why I cared. Why did it bother me so much to get the perfect statement to summarise who I was? And why was I using my job as the primary method to do so?

When I started working in the non-profit sector, I noticed a curious thing in conversations. I was constantly told by those who didn't work in the same area, "Ah, you're a good person." It didn't take long for my identity to become wrapped up in this praise.

In 2012, Paul K Piff, a social psychologist, and others, conducted an interesting study on people who drive a Prius, one of the first hybrid electric and petrol cars. Prius drivers are 1.4 times more likely to be at fault in an accident (Insurify, 2020). They analysed how likely drivers were to stop at a crosswalk and cut in front of other traffic. Prius drivers, compared to others, exhibited more selfish behaviour (Piff et al., 2012).

This behaviour has been coined "moral self-licensing" (Merritt et al., 2010), where past good deeds liberate someone from the need to act morally in the future.

"With a moral licence, it becomes increasingly difficult to make moves that are for the betterment of the cause."

You could argue that morality is at the core of the charity sector, and moral action is at the core of the worker. It isn't to say that non-profit workers drive more selfishly than others, or act more immorally. It is to say that moral self-licencing and ego can affect the way we work in the sector.

With a moral licence, it becomes increasingly difficult to make moves that are for the betterment of the cause. Instead, because we have already earned some moral credit, we might feel free to make choices that work more for ourselves (and perhaps our egos) than for the charity itself. Making a charity redundant, in this case, becomes a difficult move.

If you are able to achieve a sense of pride simply through mentioning your work, why would anyone stop this gravy train?

Feeling a sense of satisfaction is one of the key reasons why people from corporate backgrounds come to the non-profit sector to work or volunteer. This, teamed with some newly gained moral credit, can set well-intentioned people on the wrong path.

Consistent with the foreword of this book, I want to focus less on the people involved and more on how the structure of corporations and charities influences specific behaviour. And yet, when that behaviour becomes repetitive, it suggests that there's something inherent in the structure of charities that causes people to behave a certain way.

A number of years ago I was approached by a friend of a friend — let's call him Kyle — who worked for a big corporation. Our mutual friend had told Kyle that I was involved in the charity sector.

Kyle was clearly into his work at the corporation, but he felt that he wasn't contributing to a better world. He approached me to ask for advice on how he could better help people.

Kyle and I spent a good hour or two talking, and I shared my experiences of having worked for over a decade in the sector. One of the areas that seemed to hit a nerve for Kyle was the area of "voluntourism".

Voluntourism — the concept of combining travel and volunteering in a poor country like Cambodia — was increasingly popular at the time. Well-meaning Westerners spent several thousand dollars to spend a few weeks in another country, often building houses or playing with children in orphanages.

I explained why this was highly problematic. For starters, in Cambodia over 80% of the children in orphanages have parents

(Stark et al., 2017). Their parents place them in orphanages because they feel that they have better resources there. However, children who grow up in orphanages overwhelmingly face neglect, which has severe physical and mental health consequences later in life (Weir, 2014). Instead of supporting charities that help families to keep children in their homes, people volunteering in orphanages are perpetuating an often harmful system.

Kyle had considered volunteering in South-East Asia, but he seemed genuinely struck by the unintended consequences of such a trip. We discussed that it would probably be better for him to support a charity from afar — for example, by fundraising in Australia — and then taking a holiday in Asia and spending money on local businesses.

At the end of our time together, Kyle thanked me for my time and promised to keep in touch. I never heard back from him.

Just a few weeks later, though, I noticed a curious post on Kyle's Facebook. He had posted photos of his trip to South-East Asia, complete with photos of him hugging children he had just met, and with a spade in hand from some manual labour he had just completed at an orphanage.

Unsurprisingly for this kind of post, it garnered a huge amount of likes and comments, with posts ranging from simple adoration to hyperbole: "These children will never forget how much you've changed their lives!"

It was clear that despite Kyle understanding at a surface level what I had told him, he was not really ready to hear what I had to say. In fact, I now realise that our coffee meeting had no real impact on him at all.

Sometimes the desire to do good, and feel good about it, can cloud our judgment. The warm, fuzzy feelings that we get can override any rational assessment of actually contributing to improving people's lives.

As harsh as that may be to Kyle, no one is immune from this temptation, least of all myself.

As a founder of a charity, the adoration is even more extreme. You're glorified for your sacrifice. It would take the strongest of founders to not succumb to this adoration and extract your ego from your work.

Having been a founder for a number of charities and social enterprises, I have witnessed first-hand both the perks and challenges of the role. It takes a very special kind of person to want to found a charity. The self-belief that you need to have, to open yourself up to all kinds of ridicule, is something worthy of admiration.

In order to found a charity, you often cannot afford to have a shred of self-doubt in your ability to influence outcomes, such is the force required to overcome the related challenges. But therein lies the problem. One of the most important skills of a founder, and completely at odds with the kind of person who would be a founder, is the ability to let go.

You may have witnessed the founder of a charity hanging around for years after establishing it and becoming increasingly less relevant over time. It's hard to let go of something when your identity is so wrapped up within it. At an intellectual level, most founders understand that they are not just their work. But separating your identity from your work is a much harder exercise to do in practice than it is in theory.

Paternalism is rife in the charity sector

"It's incredible how competitive this industry is. People can be so cruel to one another."

This was the assessment of working in the non-profit sector by a friend of mine who had previously worked in the corporate sector. She had assumed that, coming from the private sector, non-profit workers would fulfil the stereotype of sitting around the campfire linking arms and singing 'Kum ba yah'.

She was severely disappointed.

When working together for a common cause, something strange happens when you combine ego, identity and competition. People can unite as a team, championing a cause that seems above scrutiny. The more they feel this sense of unity over a common goal, the more everyone else becomes untrustworthy.

This distrust of others sometimes even crosses over to the people that the non-profit is trying to help. A study comparing American to Australian attitudes to poverty, and who was to blame for the predicament of the poor, demonstrated a significant difference. Australians were less likely to blame poverty on the individuals themselves, compared to Americans (Feather, 1974).

Blame is a fundamentally important attitude. If we blame individuals for their own plight, it's natural to not want to empower them, but to provide solutions that are top-down. That kind of top-down solution is a breeding ground for paternalism, neo-colonialism and racism. Much has been written on how rife this is within the non-profit sector. This attitude is the birthplace of the white saviour industrial complex.

In 2012, Nigerian-American author Teju Cole took to Twitter

to respond to the then viral Kony 2012 campaign. A group called Invisible Children had released a documentary about their efforts to capture Ugandan cult leader and war criminal Joseph Kony, who amongst other things, had recruited child soldiers.

As shocking as the crime was, Cole criticised the approach taken by the white saviours. His criticism was that the approach did more to address the sentimentality of saviours than solve underlying problems with discernment.

"The White Savior Industrial Complex is not about justice. It is about having a big emotional experience that validates privilege," Cole wrote (Cole, 2012).

"When ego runs rampant within the charity sector, it's natural for focus to shift away from an outcome."

In just seven short tweets , Cole's criticism, in which even Oprah Winfrey was targeted, was shared widely. During a screening of the documentary in Northern Uganda, locals jeered and threw rocks, complaining that the film was "more about whites than Ugandans" (Bariyo & Orden, 2012).

When ego runs rampant within the charity sector, it's natural for focus to shift away from an outcome and towards the charity workers themselves.

And what happened to Invisible Children? After $30 million in funds raised and 100 million views on YouTube within five days, the goal of capturing Kony was never reached. While Kony remains at large, Invisible Children co-founder and documentary narrator, Jason Russell, penned a book about how children can run effective activism campaigns (Sanders, 2014).

One of the most obvious criticisms about Invisible Children's approach is their lack of desire to work with organisations already existing within Uganda. When acting alone, it's much easier to sell the story of the white saviour and their journey of providing hope for the "otherwise helpless Ugandans". With the white saviour mentality, taking the glory is easier when you remain sheltered from the local people of that country.

Many aid workers don't learn the local language or integrate their lifestyles into the practices of the people around them. When I worked in Cambodia, my home of five years, I'd often ask foreigners what their Khmer — the local language — was like. Far and away the most common response would be to look sheepish, avert their eyes and answer, "Oh, just terrible."

I never quite understood this attitude. People from countries like Australia or the UK would instantly assume, or even insist, that someone from Pakistan would learn English if they were to move to Australia. But there was a strange double standard when moving the other way. This creates a divide between foreign aid workers and the local people, a divide that benefits the foreigners as they exclude locals (even if it's unintentional), control the narrative and direct the flow of funding.

According to the International Federation of Red Cross, as of 2015, less than 2% of humanitarian aid goes to local NGOs (IFRC, 2015). Let's unpack this for a moment.

Of all the funding given out to NGOs in response to disasters or wars, an essentially negligible amount goes to local charities on the ground. This means that when you put your spare change into a plastic box at the supermarket, 98% of every dollar never makes it to a Nepalese charity after an earthquake, or a Syrian non-profit in response to the war.

How can this be?

As happens with growth, the larger the charities are, the more likely that they have the resources to get even more funding. The design of the charity sector simply does not favour smaller, more localised charities.

Research has shown that the smaller and younger the charity is, the more likely it is to close (Searing, 2020). Think of charities like lions in a pack. When they are in their infancy, they need nurturing and care, not to be ignored by the adult lions that overconsume the collective resources.

In recognition of this problem, the Grand Bargain: Agenda for Humanity was created out of an agreement formed at the World Humanitarian Summit in May 2016. The signatories to this agreement included entire countries (think Australia, Germany and the United States) and large international aid agencies (think Oxfam, Save the Children and UNICEF) who collectively controlled 88% of global humanitarian funding at the time (Vaessen, 2017).

One of the key goals of the Grand Bargain was to increase spending to local organisations on the ground to the ambitious target of 25% by 2020 (Agenda for Humanity, 2019). But by 2020, the proportion of direct funding to local organisations was a paltry 4% and in 2021 it halved to 2% (Metcalfe-Hough et al., 2022).

Despite best intentions, it seems genuinely difficult for the international flow of funding to go to local actors. Something structural seems to be blocking this outcome. And even when there are structural changes to the way charities operate to improve the situation, it often has unfortunate consequences.

Take Oxfam, for example. Oxfam was founded in 1942 as the Oxford Committee for Famine Relief, to help starving people in Greece after the Second World War.

In 2014, Oxfam announced that it would move its headquarters from Oxford, England, to Nairobi, Kenya (Byanyima, 2016). This followed a trend of large international charities such as ActionAid and ACORD moving their headquarters to poorer countries (Williams, 2018).

In 2014, Winnie Byanyima, the executive director of Oxfam at the time, heralded the move to shift headquarters to Kenya as a way to give counterparts from poorer countries a greater voice. By placing their head offices in Africa, they symbolically showed that they wanted to shift power to these countries.

An external study conducted in 2018 confirmed that for Oxfam, the number one driver for this change was a stronger advocacy position — that, according to Oxfam GB's Campaigns Director at the time, would enable Oxfam to "accompany people in their struggles for a fairer world"(Forsch, 2018).

Notably, the second most important driver was fundraising opportunities. An Oxfam induction pack for new staff and volunteers, titled *Oxfam 2020: Tomorrow's Oxfam Starting Today*, written in 2014, articulated the opportunity clearly: "Fundraising should be a big part of our plans as there are more and more wealthy people, corporations and foundations in emerging countries" (Oxfam International, 2014).

As large charities such as Oxfam moved to countries like Kenya, they were then able to compete with local NGOs for local funding, essentially boxing these local actors out of their potential share of resources (Bah, 2016).

How could a small grassroots charity compete with Oxfam who have scores of people working on grant writing and fundraising? It's simply not a fair fight.

It's this dynamic that further widens the resource gap between large international charities and small local charities.

"Oxfam's own policy choices have arguably created inequality in funding within the Global South."

The irony seems lost on Oxfam, who regularly campaign against widening global economic inequality, using phrases such as "economic violence" to describe structural policy choices that are "made for the richest and most powerful people" (Ahmed et al., 2022). As admirable — and unique — as this stance is, it's ironic that Oxfam produced such a campaign when their own policy choices have arguably created inequality in funding within the Global South.

Zooming out, we can see that out of the funding that governments around the world give to NGOs to develop poorer countries – otherwise known as official development assistance (ODA) – the vast majority already goes to international NGOs. Only 9% is given to NGOs from developing countries (OECD, 2014).

When local NGOs — think again of that grassroots charity in Kenya — are given funding, it is often through partnerships with larger NGOs. These larger charities will essentially outsource their work on the ground to a smaller charity that perhaps has better standing within the community.

It's great to see partnerships within the sector, but it would be even better to see small charities given agency without needing to pander to the needs and requirements of larger charities.

Whether it's a fundamental lack of trust, inability to let go, or just plain racism, this is the reality of the aid sector today. It means that for international charities, they are able to maintain their relevance and power over smaller charities. For bigger charities, they need to be needed.

We like to be needed

My first international development role was in China. A large international NGO hired me to work as an advisor at the age of 29. I was to advise national government partners on how orphanages should integrate children with disabilities into their care — no small task.

I had my own chauffeur. I was given a three-bedroom apartment all to myself, something I had never experienced in my wildly expensive hometown of Sydney. And another first — for the first time in my life, my apartment was spotless. That's because cleaning duties were no longer discharged to me, but to my own dedicated cleaner. I had a local counterpart who was on paper a project manager, but in practice spent most of his time acting as a translator for me.

In meetings with the government, I was referred to as "Professor" and was often introduced as, "One of the finest physiotherapists in the world, under the age of 30."

The reality was that while studying at university, I rarely reached higher than a credit, and that the major achievement of my actual two-year physiotherapy career was the slow recognition that I wasn't a very good physiotherapist.

I was born in Australia, where the culture values downplaying your own importance and status. The first time my colleagues called me "Professor", my instinct was to correct them.

"Oh no, I'm not a professor, I wasn't even a good student!"

But soon, another line of thinking entered my mind.

Despite us somehow engaging a high level of government, our government counterparts didn't seem to respect foreign ideas. How dare they! I had given up a year of my life to work in China and I was really trying to help those poor children in those orphanages. Respecting the agency of Chinese leadership was the last thing on my mind. One little white lie about my expertise wouldn't hurt.

After a few weeks, I stopped correcting my colleagues. Overnight, I graduated from a below average physiotherapist to one of the finest physiotherapy professors in the world.

I'm positive that this strategy occurs regularly in the charity world. Foreign 'experts' with little expertise and virtually no understanding of poverty over inflate their credentials to push their ideas onto local partners.

Before leaving Australia for China, I had been inoculated against hepatitis B, and I stayed away from mosquitos for fear of catching dengue fever. But I soon realised that I was at risk of an even greater menace. I was at risk of believing my own bullshit.

As my own ego inflated further and further and, by comparison, everyone else around me seemed incompetent, the logical conclusion is that only I could do the necessary work.

Like most things in life, it's nice to be needed.

Chapter 3

The hamster wheel

This is the hamster wheel of charity work

Landing a role in China — just shy of my thirtieth birthday — was a surreal experience. It was supposed to be my dream job. I was handed the responsibility of affecting a huge number of lives and paid handsomely to do so. I was treated like royalty.

But I soon realised that, as much as the charity had pure intentions, my main role was to keep the hamster wheel turning. Charities aren't geared to ever stop. They're geared to continue. This is what I call "the hamster wheel of charity work".

The hamster wheel is all about asking for funding, spending it and justifying why you should get more. All of a sudden, the charity's focus is no longer on the impact that they have, or even on doing a job and finishing it, but on perpetuating this cycle.

This is what is commonly referred to as the non-profit industrial complex (NPIC), a phrase first coined in the excellent book *The revolution will not be funded* to describe the relationship between business, government and non-profits, and the inevitably perverse incentives to maintain existing power structures.

In American First Nations activist Madonna Thunder Hawk's essay titled 'Native organizing before the non-profit industrial complex' — one of a series of essays in *The revolution will not be funded* — she describes the shift from a social movement to a funded non-profit.

"Once you get too structured, your whole scope changes from activism to maintaining an organization and getting paid, [and] people start seeing organizing as a career rather than as an involvement in a social movement that requires sacrifice," she lamented (Incite! Women of Color Against Violence, 2017).

"So much energy goes into the maintenance of the movement, rather than the outcomes of the movement."

The hamster wheel and NPIC are inextricably linked. So much energy goes into the maintenance of the movement, rather than the outcomes of the movement itself.

I saw both the hamster wheel and NPIC first-hand in China. We faced huge difficulties working with the Chinese government, who had made it abundantly clear that they didn't want us to tell them how to conduct their own business. I had arrived in the fifth year of a five-year project. My job was to make it look like the charity had executed their plans, to justify more funding.

But charity work, and development work in particular, rarely go to plan. In a dynamic environment, it's extremely unrealistic to plan for something that runs for as long as five years and expect it to come to fruition.

Like most projects, there had been significant delays, strong personalities to work against and some resistance from local partners. The team that I was working with was also at breaking point.

I had been brought on as an advisor to the project. In some senses, this is the best role that a foreigner can play. But from day one, staff members implored me to take over the role of project manager. That would mean usurping the position of the existing project manager, a Chinese man whose expertise was translation but had been shuffled into a managerial position once the previous manager left.

I regularly witnessed shouting and tears within the office. It was pretty clear that things weren't going well within the team.

As worryingly, to justify more funding, I was encouraged to overinflate our achievements on my evaluation report. Part of my role was to count the number of ramps that had been built within schools by local partners so that children with disabilities could access education.

Even if the actual number was below par, what difference would it make for me to round up by eight or nine here and there? No one would know the difference and, more importantly, the charity had more work to be done. By overestimating our current impact, we could justify more funding to finish the job.

But what if the job was an abject failure? What if we weren't really welcome? Maybe the best solution would be to go home and forget about the whole thing.

I'd spent years studying and volunteering to be in that situation, and I couldn't help but feel disillusioned. I found myself caught right in the middle of the hamster wheel.

Sometimes, small non-profits recognise that they can no longer continue running on the hamster wheel. Sadly, this often comes when the founder is nearing the end of their life and there's no one else able to take up the torch.

Having established a reputation as "the redundant charities guy", I'm often contacted by charity founders and board members who are interested in my advice on how to make an existing charity redundant. The intent is admirable, but practically this is very hard to do. It's very hard to turn a ship around once it's moving in a certain direction, especially if that ship is a barge in the form of a mega-NGO. Like most things, starting with the end in mind is much easier when it's done from the beginning.

This is not to say it's impossible — see Part 2 of this book.

Large non-profits have entire teams dedicated to fundraising, and just as sizeable teams on monitoring and evaluation (M&E). Many charities insist that these teams exist to understand how effective their work is. It's important that they know whether or not they're doing the right thing. But if there wasn't the added benefit of this evaluation being put to donors to receive more funding, exactly how invested in M&E would a non-profit be?

Put simply, the amount of time non-profits spend on getting and justifying funding, as opposed to doing effective work, is absurd.

Funders like to boast about how many people applied for funding, a boast which is counterproductive to what we're trying to achieve as a sector. Margaret O'Brien, CEO of the social enterprise Young Change Agents, described this common scenario via email. A foundation will give away $1 million, but because of vague criteria, might have 2,000 non-profits applying. Assuming a cost of $1,000 per non-profit in staff time spent applying for the grant, this leads to a $2 million expenditure in applications, and hence a $1 million net loss for the sector (Yeoh & O'Brien, 2022).

It seems that it's equally difficult for a donor to make themself redundant. In other words, donors need charities as much as charities need donors. As a foundation creates a structure with its own staffing, its own reporting and its own identity, it becomes equally difficult for that foundation to see itself no longer existing. This is why the concept of a redundant charity is as unnerving for a foundation as it is for a charity.

There are so many limitations on what funding can and cannot be spent on — few donors, it seems, believe that it is reasonable to spend money on management or head office costs. This is despite decades of solid arguments dispelling the myth of the overheads.

The idea that charities can confidently claim that "95% of their funding goes to the program" is unrealistic, given the lack of unstandardised measures of what an overhead is. If Oxfam moves its head office from the UK to Kenya, but it still maintains the same activities such as fundraising and management in this Kenya office, are they allowed to no longer classify expenses in Kenya as an overhead?

Most importantly, a focus on overheads is a focus on efficiency, not effectiveness. A charity can be extremely efficient in its use of funds but achieve nothing of value.

This approach means that non-profits need to find donors for niches — one for program A, one for program B, two for head office costs. This further inflates the amount of time they spend on maintaining the hamster wheel.

The pressure to gain funding is so extensive that non-profits will shift their entire focus towards areas where funding is more readily available. This practice is so common it even has a name: mission drift.

The phrase mission drift, where a charity's activities move further and further away from its original purpose, likely comes from the military phrase mission creep. First stated in 1993 in the Washington Post, mission creep was used to describe the ever-growing scope of military operations in Somalia by the United States (Hoagl, 1993).

It's fitting that the phrase mission drift may borrow from a military phrase, given the similarities between peacekeeping missions and charities. Both have a defined purpose and "enemy" and yet, as new information comes to light, there's often a temptation to increase or shift the scope of the work.

In some senses, both military operations and charity programs involve a lot of the same elements: ego and a strong need to justify existence. It's potentially why it's hard to cease a military operation once it begins. With charities, it's much the same.

The biggest issue with a focus on funding, as opposed to a focus on fixing the core problem at hand, is that it forces non-profits to focus on themselves and justify how good they are.

We lack imagination

Schopenhauer said, "Everyone takes the limits of his own vision for the limits of the world."

When a charity focuses on itself and its own limitations, the world shrinks accordingly. The non-profit will focus more and more on what they can do, rather than what is needed. They start to retrofit solutions to problems, without really taking the time to work out what the core problems are, and hence what solutions would be suitable.

If it is true that to every man with a hammer, every problem looks like a nail, then the modern non-profit wields not a hammer but a sledgehammer, beating the nail into submission until it succumbs to the force of its bludgeoning.

Amongst supermarkets, Costco is the place where every problem is solved. Need 10 litres of olive oil? No problem! Need a coffin? We've got you covered.

In the world of non-profits, the Costco equivalents are mega corporation-style non-profits like World Vision or Oxfam. They are the Swiss Army knife of social ventures. They exist to solve every problem. They've evolved over time to meet any problem that the market throws at them.

> *"They will address any multitude of problems rather than solve a central problem."*

"The market," as far as these organisations are concerned, is where funding exists. They will address any multitude of problems, assuming funding is available, rather than solve a central problem once and for all.

It's understandable that there will always be problems for large charities to address, so if they are able to continue telling their story of addressing needs, they will continue to grow. Between 1999 and 2011, World Vision increased its annual income by 365%, from US$600 million to US$2.8 billion (Forsch, 2018).

The billion-dollar revenues of mega charities are a far cry from the revenue they garnered during their humble beginnings. The first big international charities were created after the Second World War as relief efforts following the war. However, they soon evolved to serve humanitarian needs more broadly (Williams, 2018).

This is perhaps one of the first examples of mission drift. A charity starts out with a very specific purpose, which is time-bound, and then evolves to address another need. It would have been easy for the founders of these charities to justify continuing to grow. There must have been a myriad of issues in the world in the 1940s and 1950s that needed addressing.

Smaller non-profits are often born out of opportunism. Well-meaning travellers, nearing the end of their careers as teachers, will establish an organisation that teaches children English in poor countries.

This is a good example of solving a problem with the solution in mind, rather than the problem in mind. It's taking a sledgehammer to a nail, simply because that's the tool that is in one's hand.

If you are introduced to a charity by a friend, it can often be hard, without spending hours digging through annual reports, to work out if this charity is worth supporting or not. I've found that there is one shortcut that often, but not always, works to see if the charity is legit.

Scan the charity's website. Go to the 'About us' or 'History' section of the website and read about the origins of the charity. Alarm bells should ring if the origin story of the founder is something like the following:

While backpacking in Thailand, 19-year-old Chloe walked along the back streets of a poor community and was struck by the poverty the local children were facing. A young girl named Kannika, no older than eight years old, asked Chloe to buy some flowers from her. "But why aren't you in school?"

Chloe asked. Chloe gave Kannika $200 and made her vow never
to skip school again. The next day, Chloe quit her Bachelor
of Arts degree and chose to live in Thailand for the next year,
setting up a local school providing Western-standard education
for Thai children.

There is something charming about Chloe's need to act immediately, and we're instantly curious about the outcome of her story with her as the protagonist. However, as far as we can tell, Chloe has no background in social work or international development. She hasn't done any research into the root causes of Kannika's absence from school. She hasn't collaborated with any local partners.

In this example, Chloe has simply taken a sledgehammer — her good intentions and time — to the nail.

The alternative to Chloe's story can be illustrated with the well-known aphorism: give a man a fish. Upgrading to modern times, the saying goes, "Give a person a fish, and you feed them for a day. Teach a person to fish, and you feed them for a lifetime."

If we apply this thinking to the problem of lack of speech therapy in Cambodia, it becomes clear that the wisdom behind this aphorism does not apply. Keep in mind that there are no speech therapists in all of Cambodia, and yet the demand for therapy is estimated to be over half a million people. This was a situation that many well-meaning foreigners from countries like France, the United States and Australia had recognised.

Giving a person a fish in this case would mean sending across speech therapists to Cambodia to provide therapy for a few weeks a year, perhaps in their annual leave. As noble and self-sacrificing as this is, speech therapy takes weeks, if not months or years to see a difference. Providing the service for a few days in a village makes little to no difference.

Beyond this, some foreign speech therapists in Cambodia appear to have limited understanding of language, cultural considerations, history and power dynamics. They may well be excellent therapists in their home countries, but this apparent lack of contextual knowledge can significantly restrict their effectiveness in Cambodia.

These fly in fly out visits are often referred to as "missions" – an outdated word with echoes of the term "missionary". The connotations of this highly paternalistic description align with the mentality behind giving a person a fish. And yet, these missions continue to occur.

The irony of these methods of helping is that while their long term impact on the country of Cambodia is questionable, their impact on the visitors is enormous. They are very connected to the cause and quite understandably feel good about helping. Because there are tangible effects of their efforts, the effects make for great social media posts and tons of kudos.

But that's not what effective helping is about. Truly working with local partners at the forefront and supporting their needs often involves sitting in the background and not portraying yourself as an agent of change. This doesn't make for great social media posts.

While giving a person a fish is almost universally accepted as ineffective, teaching a person to fish is only marginally better.

In the context of speech therapy in Cambodia, teaching a person to fish is, for example, Australian speech therapists flying to Cambodia to conduct workshops with Cambodian health and disability workers to improve their knowledge of speech therapy. As in the first example, taking their annual leave to do so results in a couple of weeks of training per year. But as per the first example, without a grounding in context, training can only go so far.

Have you ever tried to explain something really technical about an area of interest — say, the Westminster system of government — to someone you don't know well? You would have to spend a significant amount of time understanding their level of knowledge before launching in.

The same goes for training people in a profession. And yet, with only a couple of weeks per year, there simply isn't the time to do this.

Well hang on a second, you might say. If training is so ineffective, then why do so many people request it?

This is one of the rare occasions when simply asking people what they want is not going deep enough. Put yourself in the shoes of a Cambodian community disability worker. Your job, day in, day out, is to get on a motorbike and drive long distances along dusty roads, in often 35-degree heat, to see children in their homes.

A rich Western agency is offering you the chance to sit in an air-conditioned room for a few days, with lunch supplied, and learn skills to improve your knowledge. Oh, and on top of that, they're going to be paying you a *per diem*, a daily stipend of US$20 for the inconvenience. I don't blame anyone for wanting to take up this option.

Prior to starting OIC Cambodia in 2012, there had been decades of people coming into Cambodia to provide training courses of various lengths. And still, at that stage, there was not one single Cambodian speech therapist in the country.

The issue with training is that it comes from the outside in. It's not a Cambodian-owned, Cambodian-led solution. It will always be paternalistic.

This is why to create real change in countries like Cambodia, we need to move beyond teaching a person to fish. What we need is to help Cambodia create its own fishing industry. In the case of OIC Cambodia, this is a Cambodian-owned, Cambodian-led speech therapy profession.

In practical terms, this means thinking about what is needed in a country for this to exist. Rather than thinking about what solutions a charity can offer, OIC Cambodia was started with the end in mind. We thought about the results that we wanted to have and then designed activities around them.

That's the level of clarity that a specific end goal can offer. It avoids all debate around mission drift. As opportunities come up to do specific pieces of work, all anyone needs to ask to determine if it's appropriate or not is, "Does this piece of work get us any closer to our end point?"

Something is better than nothing

"Well, you know. Something is better than nothing, right?"

This is the fundamental attitude of many non-profits and well-meaning volunteers entering poorer countries. It's the default argument for providing something, even if the end goal isn't ever apparent.

In 2013, after just arriving in Cambodia, I was in contact with an American company that helps connect busy professionals to volunteering opportunities across the world. According to their website, the founder of the company once lamented that there were no volunteering opportunities globally that would let her volunteer for one week — they all required a longer commitment. If ever there was an example of focusing on the hammer, with the nail as an afterthought, this is it. Hence, the "voluntourism" company was born.

I stumbled on the company after discovering that children with disabilities in rural Cambodia had been supplied wheelchairs by travelling volunteers. The design of the wheelchairs had been deliberately simplified so that they could be assembled by their American volunteers in a fly-in fly-out visit to Cambodia. These volunteers paid over a thousand dollars for a one week trip to Cambodia to assemble and gift these wheelchairs in "wheelchair parties".

The first thing I noticed about these wheelchairs was that they were adult sized. But, in communication with the founder, she was insistent that the recipients of these wheelchairs had to be children, since the volunteers found working with children more gratifying.

Putting my physio hat on, there were inherent issues with the design. The seat was essentially an adult sized chair — think of a cheap $10 plastic chair from your local hardware store — that would not fit many children below adolescence. These children often had muscular weakness and couldn't sit independently, so they needed more supportive seating, not rigid plastic adult-sized chairs.

Beyond being uncomfortable, it could pose a safety risk if they were to fall out of the chair and injure themselves.

Putting my charity hat on, as the wheelchairs were made with foreign parts and assembled by foreign people, the chairs would be almost impossible for local people to fix. The wheelchairs were also brittle, and as they were made of cheap plastic, they couldn't handle the bumpy roads in Cambodia and would often break. Finally, after speaking with local staff, they reported that the most common use for this wheelchair was not as an assistive device for mobility, but as a piece of furniture.

Besides which, the whole concept of a Western company, which makes money out of voluntourism opportunities, trying to find people to retrofit their solution to already feels unethical.

I reached out to the founder of this company and suggested another alternative — have the volunteers purchase locally made and sourced wheelchairs instead. She insisted that if they could have a hand in assembling these wheelchairs, it would really help to "light a fire" under the volunteers. The founder made a point that she was open to any opportunities that *nonskilled* (emphasis hers) volunteers could be part of. Regardless of the suitability of the wheelchair design to local people, it appeared that the needs of American volunteers were more important.

The notion that "something is better than nothing" is pervasive in international charity work. It's why speech therapists trained in Australia, with no development experience, Cambodian language knowledge or understanding of Cambodian culture and history, can fly from Australia to Cambodia to perform speech therapy in a Cambodian village.

It's why white volunteers can walk into an orphanage full of vulnerable children, without so much as a child protection check, and hug them. Physically touch them, without a shred of doubt.

It's why non-profits can spend millions of dollars sending substandard equipment overseas, equipment that is falling apart and unable to be repaired in-country because the parts or knowledge to do so do not exist locally.

The "something is better than nothing" mentality allows us to drop our standards to a level that wouldn't be acceptable anywhere else. It's a key factor in perpetuating the hamster wheel of non-profit work.

We focus on quantitative outputs, known as vanity metrics in other industries, because it suits this style of work. It allows us to say, "Because of us, 100 children received wheelchairs from us last year!"

And when someone dares to ask the most important questions like, "But even if 100 children received wheelchairs, were they using them one year later?" the answer is, "Well, you know. Something is better than nothing, right?"

Chapter 4

When there's
no end point

There's no true empowerment

Nowhere in the design of a non-profit is there an incentive to finish a job or solve a problem. Non-profits are designed to self-perpetuate.

In his excellent book, *Winners take all*, Anand Giridharadas describes how the helping sector prefers using the word 'poverty' over 'inequality'. In funding applications, it's far more common to see the word 'poverty' than the word 'inequality'.

Quoting Bruno Giussani, a curator of TED, "Poverty is essentially a question that you can address via charity ... A person of means, seeing poverty, can write a check and reduce that poverty" (Giridharadas, 2018).

Poverty is something that is actionable. It is something that can be addressed with the flourish of a signature and the mailing of a cheque.

Inequality, on the other hand, is about changing the system. It's also about looking at those who are in positions of power and how they contributed to inequality in the first place. This includes those self-appointed with fixing the problem: foundations.

In 'Democratizing American philanthropy', another short essay from *The revolution will not be funded*, by Christine Ahn, she argues that foundations do little towards affecting social change. Rather, because wealthy people are exempt from paying taxes when they start a foundation, they are essentially given a free pass on money that the public is owed. Instead of this money being used by democratically elected officials to create a better society, it is instead used at the behest of individuals who have often become rich through exploiting less wealthy workers.

In their preference to address poverty instead of inequality, foundations maintain the status quo and keep themselves in a position to be needed. Power structures don't change.

As charities are often slaves to the whims of foundations, they too get caught up in this pattern. For charities, there's a fervour to keep on doing, to get more funding and to grow bigger and bigger.

Without a plan to leave, the design of the charity's work is short-term and flawed. Nothing demonstrates this more than Plan International's abrupt exit from Sri Lanka. After working in Sri Lanka for four decades, Plan International announced it was leaving Sri Lanka as the country had made significant gains in economic growth and standards of living (McVeigh, 2021). Child sponsorship was approximately a third of Plan's income in 2020–21 (Plan International, 2022). These days child sponsorship is not necessarily just money that goes directly to a family, it is money that is directed to a community for a very specific purpose. In Plan's case in Sri Lanka, donors were told they had two weeks to write goodbye letters to the children they had sponsored and were offered children in other countries to support (McVeigh, 2021). The hamster wheel must, at all costs, keep on turning.

The most unsatisfying part of this story is the lack of information about what happened in Sri Lanka after Plan International left. What happened to the children whose education was half funded? Did they drop out of school? Were the families able to continue sustaining themselves once support was withdrawn or were they set up to fail?

Like Plan, once the monitoring and evaluation teams withdrew, we will simply never know.

In 2017, the US foreign aid department funded a report investigating the reasons behind non-profits exiting developing

> *"What happened to the children whose education was half funded? Did they drop out of school?"*

countries (Leach, 2018). There were two major reasons why aid exits occurred. The first: because the project ran out of money. The second: because the donor government decided that it didn't want to work with the host government any longer.

Neither of these reasons involve planning with local partners to ensure continuity exists when the non-profit exits. Neither of these reasons set the country up for success.

For an international charity to exit successfully, one of the factors that must remain is a strong local civil society network. But international charities outcompete local charities in almost every way. When they leave, a weak civil society remains.

One of the ways international charities outcompete local

charities is through salary. In-country, there is often a pay gap between foreign and local staff, for essentially the same roles. It's therefore impossible for local staff to have an equal footing with their foreign counterparts. Often, this pay gap is justified by higher expenses that foreigners have, including quality of life or mortgages that they have to pay in their home countries.

A 2014 salary study in Cambodia found that large international charities pay top tier staff three times more than equivalent staff in local Cambodian charities of the same size (Cooperation Committee for Cambodia, 2014). The most capable Cambodian staff, who speak the best English, leave local grassroots organisations for better paying jobs within international charities.

It's unsurprising that international charities and UN agencies, with the most resources, attract even more resources and dictate how development work is done. Even if they partner with local grassroots charities to implement projects, they still benefit from a massive power imbalance.

And what happens when, like Plan International in Sri Lanka, the international charity decides to exit in a hurry? It creates chaos.

Within international charities themselves, the very opposite of the structure that would be required to enable redundancy exists. In order to make themselves redundant, international charities need local people in positions of power who understand the local context and can manage the process of becoming redundant.

But as the heads of international non-profits are often white, this creates a serious problem — local people in poorer countries never get a chance to solve problems for themselves. There's no true empowerment.

In extreme examples, large charities like Caritas will have

hundreds of staff based in Australia and fly them out for 'monitoring' trips, while attempting to maintain control over projects that occur on the other side of the world. This outdated model means that local staff are never truly in a position of power.

Though things are definitely changing in this regard, it's still common for local people to make up the majority of the workforce in an international charity but be virtually non-existent in leadership roles.

When I lived in Cambodia, a well-regarded French-founded charity had not one single Cambodian person in the leadership team.

Without true empowerment of local leadership, a non-profit has no chance of ever saying goodbye successfully. Much like a parent who coddles their child, many international non-profits refuse to let go and risk not being needed.

We can't move on

When a charity doesn't have a distinct end point, other causes get missed. Championing their one singular cause takes precedence over all others. The charity doubles-down on their cause, attracting more resources at the cost of others potentially more worthy causes.

If you Google "NGO exit strategies," there are surprisingly few hits. It's not a topic at the forefront of many people's minds. However, one of those hits might be a discussion in the Cambodian publication, the *Phnom Penh Post*, in 2014 amongst charities about when the appropriate time to exit Cambodia would be. A number of NGOs, including Oxfam, led the discussion, encouraging international NGOs to exit. However, Chris Macqueen, Director of Strategy and Evidence at World Vision, disagreed. His argument was that it was too early to consider exiting, quoting an impressive list of metrics around poor malnutrition, child labour and illiteracy (Ponniah, 2014).

This one argument illustrates the myopia of large international NGOs. You wouldn't drive to a multi-day hike across a mountain range only to consider the road or sleeping conditions midway through. You would ensure the car was suited to the road you were about to traverse, and that the equipment you had packed suited the environment. All this happens before you leave.

Using the logic that 'the world is a mess, give us more money to fix it' is not only self-defeating, because there will be no incentive to actually fix the core issue, but it is also nonsensical. There will always be problems to fix in the world. The key question is, what are you doing to ensure these problems are addressed, once and for all?

If charities wait for problems to be solved before thinking about moving on, they'll be waiting forever. In the US, there's an incredibly inspiring charity called the Wounded Warrior Project. This cause satisfies almost all of the requirements to be described as 'a good cause'.

The Wounded Warrior Project helps returned veterans by providing services and through advocating for change. With a score of 86 out of 100 on Charity Navigator in 2019, donors can be assured that their donations are being used prudently.

Putting aside obvious points around the United States' approach to health care, how is it that this cause is not something funded by the US government? If the US government decides to send off its own citizens to fight a war and they then return with needs, you would expect the government to be the one to provide for them.

The fact that the charity is able to raise US$287 million a year to cover this gap is indicative of the fact that there is a gap in services provided by the government (Wounded Warrior Project, 2021).

Although the Wounded Warrior Project does advocate for change within the government, this is a small portion of their work. Approximately 3% of their expenditure goes towards 'government relations', whereas the vast majority goes towards programs, including mental health, financial wellness and providing veterans opportunities to connect. In other words, 97% of their work involves addressing symptoms of the problem, through providing programs, while 3% is addressing the root cause.

The Wounded Warrior Project is an excellent example of a valuable service to the community. It feels like the kind of cause that is above criticism, until you ask the question: what is the end point?

To oversimplify, if the Wounded Warrior Project flipped its proportion of work and spent 97% of its funding on advocating for change within the government, it may well have a shot at becoming redundant.

Too many causes have too many resources, whereas some have none. But it's not for a lack of resources in the world that we can't solve problems, it's a lack of focus.

One area that illustrates this well is through the existence of neglected tropical diseases (NTDs), a group of diseases that can lead to severe disability or death. Not insignificant in number, a full one billion of the world's poorest people are infected with at least one NTD (Hotez et al., 2009). Despite this, it's widely accepted that a focus on HIV/AIDS, malaria and tuberculosis — the so-called big three — has led to proportionally less funding on NTDs (Feasey et al., 2010). This misalignment is significant. Despite the heavy burden of disability worldwide, NTDs receive about 0.6% of overseas aid budgets, compared to HIV/AIDS (30 to 40%), tuberculosis (1.3 to 3.4%) and malaria (2.4 to 5.3%) (Payne & Fitchett, 2010).

In the non-profit sector, we prefer to focus on short-term wins. It's much easier to report progress, especially when donors want reports every six months. The six-month timeframe is often far too short to achieve real progress, but if it keeps funding alive, non-profits will play the game. Collectively, the charity sector has seemingly agreed to focus on short-term metrics. But when we focus on the wrong metrics, it's impossible for us to move on. This is a classic example of groupthink. To illustrate this point, we can look a little further to the animal kingdom, and the behaviour of an imaginary group of monkeys.

We're focussing on the wrong metrics

Let's imagine there are five monkeys in a room. At the top of a ladder is a basket full of bananas. One monkey climbs the ladder and attempts to reach the bananas, but as it does so, all the monkeys in the room get sprayed by cold water. The scientists pull that monkey out of the room and replace it with another.

The new monkey sees the bananas and also attempts to climb the ladder. Oh no you don't, the other four monkeys think. They've seen how this ends and they're not up for getting sprayed with cold water again. The four veteran monkeys pull the newbie down as quickly as they can. One by one, another monkey from the original five is replaced by a new monkey, until all five monkeys in the room have never witnessed anyone being sprayed by cold water.

Despite this, each new monkey that attempts to climb the ladder is yanked down by the other monkeys.

This anecdote, told by Bryan Johnson, the founder of the payment platform Braintree, is an excellent example of learnt behaviour (Daniel, 2021). It has become accepted that climbing the ladder isn't a good idea, even though no one has proof that there will be negative consequences. None of the monkeys has the courage to challenge the status quo.

In the non-profit sector, the status quo is a focus on short-term, meaningless metrics. This is the accepted behaviour that indicates success or failure. Often quantitative, none of these metrics say anything about the impact that a charity has in creating meaningful change in the community.

As we are bombarded with more and more information every day, our ability to focus on new information gets shorter and shorter. In 2013, a Twitter global trend would last for an average of 17.5 hours. In 2016, this Twitter trend lasted for only 11.9 hours (McClinton, 2019).

Even non-fiction books are getting shorter and shorter (the irony!) as our attention spans decrease. Between 2011 and 2017, the average non-fiction best seller dropped 42% in length (Max, 2017). There's no doubt that our ability to be patient is getting poorer and poorer.

The same is true in the non-profit sector. Accepted timelines to deliver results are shortening. It is not uncommon for a charity to have to scope out a community, do a needs assessment, come up with a plan in consultation with said community, deliver the plan and evaluate the (hopefully highly successful) intervention — all within 12 months.

By comparison, it took Twitter, the social network giant with over 300 million users worldwide, 12 full years to become profitable.

A number of companies, such as Tesla, which has been around for 16 years, are yet to become profitable. It seems that the patience shown by investors in high-risk for-profit companies is not replicated by funders in non-profits.

In the charity world, our measures of success are not only short-term, they are also shallow. How many wells did the charity dig this year? How many girls went to school?

These short-term, quantitative approaches are easy to capture and easy to communicate. But things get murky once we start to engage with complexity.

Who is going to maintain the wells once they are dug? Are they valued? When the girls went to school, how were their lives changed? Did the school accept them into the school year because they felt morally compelled to, or because of the possibility of funding being attached? Most importantly, what happens to the wells and girls once the charity leaves?

Under a system that measures such short-term success, what incentive is there for a charity to even think of leaving?

Out of all the metrics, the most meaningless is one often quoted by charities — the amount of money raised. It speaks to the inputs in a project but says nothing about the outputs produced.

It would be like a marathon runner talking about how many carbohydrates were consumed before a race, rather than the time or distance achieved.

Most non-profit workers know that these metrics are meaningless. They're not clueless. But they choose to keep talking about them because it's what the donors and the public want to hear. Much like the five monkeys, it's easy to continue playing the charade that is the status quo.

Imagine if we looked beyond the 10 or 25 years that a charity works in an area, to the millennia that occur after the charity leaves.

Charity Success

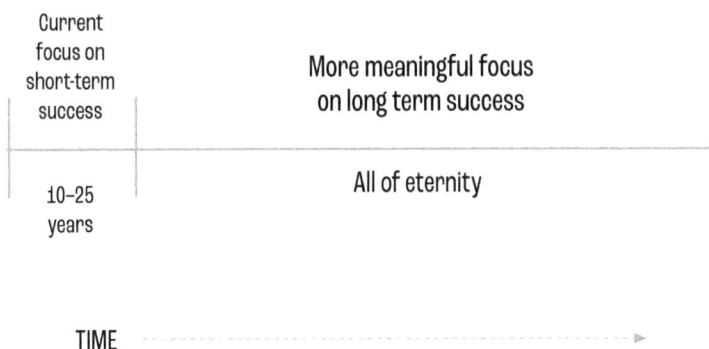

Current focus on short-term success	More meaningful focus on long term success
10–25 years	All of eternity

TIME ➤

Thinking of charity this way changes our entire concept of success. And therefore, it changes the way charities report. It would require donors to stop asking: "How many wells did the charity dig this year? How many girls went to school?"

It would require donors to start asking: "What milestones have you hit this year to make yourself redundant?"

Working in this way would involve courage, curiosity and self-awareness.

Fortunately, there are good examples of charities with this mindset. The remainder of this book will explore charities across the spectrum, from those who have already made themselves redundant, to those along the journey, to those grappling with the transition from a traditional charity to a redundancy model.

Part 2

How to Set Up a Redundant Charity

Chapter 5

Defining an end point

How to clarify an end point

There are a number of non-profits redefining what success looks like. They're modern in their approach. They're humble, curious and self-aware. They demonstrate an incredible level of open-mindedness. No longer satisfied with the status quo, they challenge themselves to go further. Finally, they're diverse: they break the mould of the stereotypical white, privileged non-profit worker.

Unlike standard models of non-profits detailed earlier in this book, they focus far more on being useful than on themselves. They are a new generation of redundant charities.

When you talk to a redundant charity leader, it's immediately clear that the way they think about the world is different. They would feel too embarrassed to boast about where they are expanding to, or how much money they've raised.

They're more concerned with questions like: "What are the results we're seeking? What's the endpoint? What happens after?"

Rather than focusing on the success of the non-profit within its short lifespan, they focus on the legacy that the organisation leaves behind. After all, lifespan is measured in decades. Legacy is measured in centuries, if not millennia.

In answering the question "What happens after?" redundant charities are aware that there are four typical outcomes:

1. The charity hands its work over to government

2. The charity hands its work over to a local NGO or civil society organisation (CSO)

3. The charity creates a vacuum filled by a private sector solution

4. The charity has solved the problem and doesn't need to hand anything over

In the next few chapters, I'll showcase how these redundant charities are achieving these four outcomes.

In this chapter I'll cover the story of Splash, one of the few charities that are intentionally leaving countries and publicly talking about why this is a better model. I will also profile Solomon King and his charity, Fundi Bots, in Uganda. Solomon's story covers his struggle with resisting the urge to grow too rapidly.

In Chapter 6, I'll look at the stories of WaterSHED and OIC Cambodia, both working to effect change through working within government. I'll also cover the work of Global Water 2020, who solved their problem effectively through advocacy, and didn't need to hand over anything as their goal was achieved. Finally, I'll introduce you to Womena, working to stimulate private sector demand for menstrual products in Uganda.

In Chapter 7, I will profile a group in the UK preparing people to end their program, particularly from an emotional point of view. I'll also cover Raising the Village, working with local civil society in the same country. Finally, I'll profile Water for People who are using spreadsheets to defy stereotypes of amateur non-profit work.

* * *

Eric Stowe of Splash

Standing at six foot four, Eric Stowe looks like your typical ex-college quarterback from any number of cheesy Hollywood movies. He speaks loudly and confidently. Eric had worked in social justice and the orphanage ecosystem for five years before founding Splash, a charity set up to provide clean water to children. Eric saw that the problems in orphanages were also endemic in schools and hospitals and realised that no one was creating a scalable solution. As an ambitious and energetic young founder, Eric immediately set out trying to expand and scale the organisation in as many countries as possible.

The Eric of that era is very different from the Eric of today. For starters, Eric now speaks proudly of the fact that Splash has shrunk. The charity had previously worked in eight countries, but now works in only two. Eric discovered that providing clean drinking water was easy, but that 50% of projects failed in the first two years. Rather than expansive, short-term wins, Eric discovered that real change occurred when behaviour change was driven through a more considered approach.

As Eric says in his TEDx talk titled 'How to Kill Your Charity (Yes, That's A Good Thing)', "Charity is a means, it cannot be the end" (Stowe, 2013).

In drawing from the Martin Luther King Jr quote, "The arc of the moral universe is long, but it bends toward justice," Eric notes that charities are not built to last the distance but are fleeting by nature. To ensure justice, Eric insists, the charity must die.

This mindset has enabled Splash to successfully leave Ethiopia, where the government co-funded water projects. Splash is now contributing to something bigger than themselves. One key way they have managed to do this is through focussing on the end point.

Ethiopia is something of a success story for Eric and his team. But it hasn't all been roses for Splash. In fact, in a way that is refreshing in the non-profit sector, Eric is clear that Nepal is where Splash has failed.

While donors were lining up to fund Splash's work in Nepal, Eric says the Nepalese government wasn't willing to co-fund, and hence, their work had limited long-term impact and was essentially a failure.

So, what was different in Ethiopia? For starters, when Splash approached a city government in Ethiopia, the discussion was incredibly transparent from the get-go.

The team at Splash had done an incredible amount of preparation for their first meeting. They had performed diagnostics in every school in the city, and even knew better than the government how many children were in the schools, what the water quality was like and the conditions of the toilets.

Having done this groundwork, they then told the government that it would cost US$20 million for every school to have sustainable water and sanitation, and that they would either have to front up US$6.2 million or Splash would walk away. In the end, the government counterparts produced US$10 million of funding for a project that will eventually cost US$25 million. Splash worked with this government to monitor progress. In the meantime, another city

"Splash is undergoing a three-year plan to have Splash Ethiopia become financially independent and purely autonomous"

government came forward and wanted much of the same, fronting up US$4 million.

In contrast to so many in the charity world who give in to their desire to be needed, there's plenty to admire about the way Splash drew a line in the sand in Ethiopia, and refused to cross it.

The success of the model in Ethiopia doesn't end there. Much like a mothership with autonomous satellites shooting off around it, Splash is undergoing a three-year plan to have Splash Ethiopia become financially independent and purely autonomous, as a condition to retain the Splash brand. This would require the Ethiopian government to fund 50 to 75% of the upfront costs, and 100% of the tail end costs of the project.

It's fascinating to see the evolution of Splash from a stock-standard charity providing water, sanitation and hygiene (WASH) solutions, to working heavily with the government to convince them to fund this need, to taking an arm's length approach and having the government ultimately fund projects themselves.

Eric may look like he's the kind of guy who is comfortable in the locker room, but he says the most effective non-profits act more like the conductor of an orchestra than a quarterback, helping local people design a model that suits their needs and desires.

It's an approach that has enabled them to create something greater than themselves in Ethiopia.

Resist the growth obsession

"When I was a child, the quality of education in Uganda progressively got worse compared to previous decades," Solomon King tells me via video call. "It got worse when the government introduced universal primary and secondary education. The focus on an increase in enrolment eventually led to a significant decrease in quality and consistency of learning."

In 1997, the President of the Republic of Uganda, Mr Yoweri Kaguta Museveni, announced that primary school education would be free for up to four children per household (Kan & Klasen, 2020). Solomon King was 14 years old. Ten years later, universal secondary education was announced (Kakuba et al., 2021).

Solomon tells me that the push for universal education resulted in a huge influx of students into the system — a system that was already fragile and not coping. "Children were being pushed through the system purely to just pass onto the next grade," Solomon says.

"Teachers were basically rushing through the curriculum, students were being tasked to memorise information instead of understanding. But when the exam is done, students wouldn't even remember what they studied."

The evidence seems to back up Solomon's perspective: the policy was more about metrics that looked good, as opposed to improved quality. It's ironic that Solomon's story originates from a vanity metric, something incredibly common in the charity space.

Ever since he was a young boy, Solomon was always curious. Born in Northern Uganda, he moved with his family to Central Uganda, to a small town named Lugazi, when he was six.

As a child of the 1990s, there was very little TV available, and certainly no internet. Solomon struggled to find outlets to satisfy his curiosity.

By the time he reached secondary school, Solomon had hit a growth spurt and was tall and wiry. He was excited at the prospect of learning in the physics, biology and chemistry labs of King's College, Budo. Unfortunately, he couldn't find anything to satisfy his curiosity there either.

It seemed that the teaching methodology of secondary school was as rote-based as in primary school. It seemed that the *modus operandi* of the school was to simply have students pass exams. But Solomon wasn't interested in just being another student in this factory of students.

One day while browsing through the library, Solomon found a book called *The Engineer in Wonderland* by an author named ER Laithwaite, and his mind was blown.

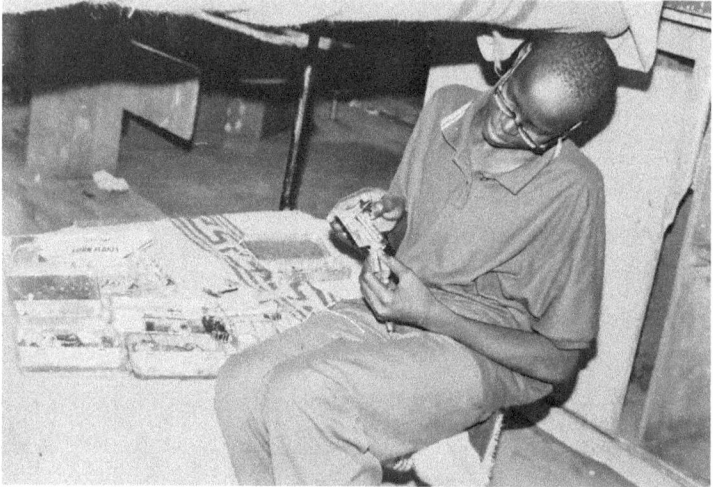

Solomon at age 13 experimenting in his school dorm

The book captures a series of lectures by Eric Laithwaite, professor of heavy electrical engineering at Imperial College. In it, he recounts running a number of science experiments for secondary students, including a whole series focussing on object levitation. For Solomon, the book captured the essence of discovery and practicality missing in the Ugandan science curriculum.

Solomon excitedly brought the book to his science teacher, asking if they could go through it in class. The answer was a resounding "no". The book was not in the curriculum.

Solomon credits this experience as the catalyst for founding Fundi Bots in 2011, a social enterprise in Uganda that provides hands-on scientific learning. Fundi Bots works within African

Solomon King of Fundi Bots

schools, with a strong focus on rural and underprivileged regions and a push for equitable inclusion for girls.

As a child, Solomon himself displayed curiosity and a desire to push back on the status quo. As an adult, he's no different.

Solomon himself has had to grapple with the growth obsession that almost all charities face. Even though the Fundi Bots website has an ambitious goal to reach *1 million African youth by 2030*, Solomon believes that growth for growth's sake is pointless.

"I've walked away from several potential donor partnerships because of how fast they wanted us to grow," says Solomon. "Fast growth would have been detrimental to our work."

How then does Solomon deal with the fact that on the face of it, Fundi Bots looks like any other charity with a mission to implement and a mission to grow?

"We've always known that our key challenge will be figuring out how to engage the government from the beginning," says Solomon. "The problem is though, for the government to change anything, you need to have high-quality evidence. And high-quality evidence only comes through an extended evaluation."

Traditional charities see the effect of their program as their end game. They have managed to improve people's lives. The team at Fundi Bots recognise that hundreds and thousands of children have benefitted from their work. But, this isn't the end game for them.

> *"We've always known that our key challenge will be figuring out how to engage the government from the beginning."*

As gratifying as it is to see children educated in a way that Solomon wasn't, this program is there to demonstrate to the government the value of practical, hands-on, scientific education. "We work with the Ministry of Education, the Regional District Education officers and the National Curriculum Development Centre who set the curriculum. So, it's pretty centred around eventual adoption by the government at some point," Solomon tells me.

Once Fundi Bots is able to demonstrate this program well enough, while avoiding the temptation to scale for the sake of it, the organisation will be in a position to make itself redundant. It's an ambitious dream.

So given all of this, when does Solomon think that Fundi Bots can actually close its doors? "I think the ideal scenario would be to tell African governments that 'Look, this model works and it can be implemented effectively and efficiently. Please take it and run with it.' At that point, Fundi Bots will likely pivot to focus on technology research (commercially) or may have an education institution of its own."

Make sure the end point is SMART

Without a deadline, non-profits, like human beings, drift on for all eternity.

If you studied at university, you were probably told over and over again about the importance of SMART goals. Goals should be specific, measurable, achievable, realistic and timebound. A redundant charity is one that uses SMART goals and then keeps on talking about them, insisting that the charity should be held accountable.

The organisations I spoke to differed in how they viewed end points, but they all agreed on one thing. The end point had to be time bound.

While many non-profits talk about the vague notion of "working themselves out of a job", very few are able to say that they will achieve this by a specific date.

Think about it. See if you can name more than a couple of charities who clearly state this timeframe. I'd be surprised if you could name one. This, in and of itself, is a radical move that separates redundant charities from the pack.

For Geoff Revell, founder of WaterSHED, a charity that was based in Cambodia to create market solutions in the water, sanitation and hygiene (WASH) sector, the time period was 10 years. This was a sufficient time frame to signal to the Cambodian government their intention to build their capacity, then step away. Revell is one of very few people in the world who can claim to have successfully initiated and completed a non-profit program internationally. He told me that setting hard deadlines was imperative to avoid shifting goal posts.

So how clear should those goal posts be? How specific should SMART goals be that are conditional to achieving exit?

In the case of WaterSHED, not specific at all. Revell is a big believer in unconditional exits (Revell, 2021). This means the 10-year timeframe is completely arbitrary, and the non-profit has little to no idea about what result will exist by the end of it. The advantage of an unconditional exit is that it puts the onus on local partners — in WaterSHED's case, private sector and government — to plan for the future themselves. In contrast to traditional non-profits, it requires WaterSHED to no longer be needed.

This approach contrasts with Water for People, another WASH charity headquartered in the United States, who take an extremely detailed approach involving the use of checklists that are developed with local partners (Water for People, 2018). In email correspondence, Kimberley Lemme, Water for People's Director of Program Learning and Influence, argued that this detailed approach, driven by discussions with local partners, ensured that the correct time frame was set by the people on the ground, and that conditions were adequate for a smooth exit. Both approaches are logical, and most importantly, the logic is driven by the need to give local people power in decision-making.

Marianne Tellier is the co-founder of Womena, a non-profit promoting the use of menstrual cups in Uganda. She initially set a timeline of five years for her non-profit to achieve exit but had to extend it to 15 years. This shouldn't come as a surprise to anyone who knows a founder.

Founders are visionaries. They see things as achievable in timeframes that others see as impossible. It's fitting that the initial timeline set by a founder is too optimistic.

With OIC Cambodia, while the project was started in 2013, we only decided on our deadline a year later. We wanted to ensure that we focussed on what had to remain in Cambodia for speech therapy as a profession to exist. Using some very simple calculations, based upon the number of speech therapists per capita in the United States, we estimated that we needed approximately 6,000 speech therapists in Cambodia to service the population.

Getting to 6,000 would take several lifetimes and wasn't a viable end point in the near future. We then thought of a point in time where we had significant momentum to get to the 6,000, and where, if the charity exited, the Cambodian government and society could take over the responsibility of growing the profession for themselves.

We thought that if we had 100 speech therapists, and if they were working in the public sector, that would signify a point in time where enough momentum had gathered. We then estimated that we could achieve this by 2030.

From there, our own SMART goal was established: OIC Cambodia would exit Cambodia in 2030 when there were 100 speech therapists integrated into the public sector.

While each redundant charity differs in their exact approach, what binds them together is a willingness to go far beyond typical non-profit rhetoric to "no longer be needed". The first step for a charity to become redundant is to set a realistic deadline and then, as much as possible, stick to it.

Chapter 6

Defining an exit strategy

Redefine what success looks like

Cambodia isn't the ideal country for a redundant charity. This is a country that had not only experienced civil war, but also the ignominy of the United Nations coming in and forming a transitional government in 1992. After a long history of colonialism under its belt, Cambodia once again found itself "saved" by foreign influences. The 'gold rush' of UN agencies and NGOs that followed was overwhelming. At one point, Cambodia had the second highest number of NGOs per capita in the world (Domashneva, 2013).

Most non-profits need to partner with the government to do anything sustainable. Given the proliferation of NGOs in Cambodia, getting the government's attention involved a fair amount of jostling and often came down to answering the question: "Who is going to pay more?"

For government officials, there is an allure to receiving multi-day training sessions by foreign experts. Government staff had grown an unhealthy appetite for *per diems* — stipends paid daily to attend these workshops in lieu of their normal work — and lunches that were supplied.

Holding a workshop at the Intercontinental Hotel? Okay, we're potentially interested.

Paying a *per diem* of $40 a day? Well, that pales in comparison to Oxfam who are paying $80. Do you think you can raise it?

This is what makes Sovattha Neou, the eventual Executive Director of WaterSHED's story even more fascinating.

Sovattha is an incredibly engaging Cambodian woman. When I spoke to her, she had angled her webcam upwards towards the ceiling in a deliberate attempt to hide the fact that she was juggling minding her own children and full-time work. Like many highly adaptive Cambodian people I had met, Sovattha's path to working in the non-profit sector was hardly linear. She had studied agriculture, then graduated as a veterinarian, then worked as a translator before returning to complete her Master of agriculture.

Sovattha Neou, the Executive Director of WaterSHED

After 15 years of working with NGOs, she had come to accept that bidding for government attention with cash was a reality. So, when she interviewed for a role with WaterSHED, she was surprised to learn that WaterSHED didn't pay government partners to be trained; the government partners actually paid for the workshops themselves. Not only that, but the program she was interviewing for would intentionally end.

When we spoke, Sovattha admitted to me that she had misunderstood this. It wasn't just that the program she was to be hired into would end. In fact, the entire charity would shut down, a far more difficult task to execute.

"she had come to accept that bidding for government attention with cash was a reality."

Sovattha had always excelled at her study and work, and had her pick of career options. Her family had encouraged her to create her own NGO so she could be self employed for the rest of her life. They actively discouraged her to work for a local NGO as it didn't have the glamour of a World Vision or a Plan International. But a charity that had somehow worked out how to get governments to pay for their own training? This was intriguing. She accepted the job offer.

How did WaterSHED achieve this feat that very few non-profits do in Cambodia, and how did they eventually manage to exit?

One answer is through the use of graduation schemes. By framing a potential negative — foreign assistance will end — into a positive, they were able to shift the mindsets of their local partners. More than

2,000 local leaders were put through the Civic Champions program, a peer-to-peer program where officials planned and actioned goals set within their own communities (WaterSHED, 2021). The Civic Champions program created something for local government that most foreign NGOs were unable to: ownership.

Think of it from the Cambodian government's perspective. If charities are bidding for your attention to solve your own problems for you, this isn't exactly conducive to ownership.

When a senior official in the Cambodian government expressed concern over WaterSHED's exit, this is how a deputy provincial governor responded: "We are not children. We can lead this now" (Revell, 2021).

Geoff and Sovattha at a public meeting in
Sihanoukville, Cambodia

WaterSHED managed to tap into a universal value: pride. By framing their exit as an opportunity for local officials to exercise their own power, the team was able to redefine success.

We need to redefine success in the non-profit sector. And we can start by redefining what we measure as success.

There's an old management adage: "What gets measured gets managed." But if we don't measure the right things, we can never achieve a good outcome.

As discussed in Part 1 of this book, traditional non-profits use measurements of success that are meaningless and short-term. Redundant charities measure things that matter.

Therein lies the inherent tension between the old and the new. This tension was palpable when I sought funding for OIC Cambodia.

Funding bodies in Cambodia wanted the non-profit to show how it was achieving impact right then and there. How many children had received speech therapy? How many people have now been able to find jobs due to speech therapy?

These metrics are meaningful to people at a given point in time, but they don't indicate long-term success. But funding bodies aren't used to measuring success any differently, and they're certainly not used to NGOs telling them how it should be done.

Slowly but surely, this is changing, particularly amongst smaller funding bodies. In conversations with some small family foundations, there's a desire to listen and adapt to a new way of viewing charities. Some donors are starting to see the benefit of viewing charities through a lens of redundancy.

After years of leading a charity and pleading with donors to embrace redundancy, I finally had the chance to walk the talk myself when it became my time to play the role of donor.

In 2017, four years after starting OIC Cambodia and with five years of living in Cambodia, I handed off the leadership of the organisation to Chenda Net, a Cambodian woman with vast experience in the development sector in Cambodia. At the time of writing, she is still leading the organisation in-country.

A couple of years after moving back to Australia, I set up OIC Australia, a non-profit organisation that existed purely to fund OIC Cambodia. I wanted OIC Australia to have a different relationship to OIC Cambodia than a traditional funder would.

"Current perspectives of success focus on a snapshot in time, redundant charities focus on the legacy that the organisation is leaving behind"

For one, OIC Australia was not a head office of any kind. It wasn't there to tell OIC Cambodia how to do program work. And it certainly wasn't there to tell OIC Cambodia how to measure success.

One of the ways in which OIC Australia operates differently to a traditional funder was through discarding short-term measures of success. Rather than asking OIC Cambodia how many children had received speech therapy, it was able to ask the more important question: "What progress has been made towards exit?"

At the time of writing this book, both OIC Cambodia's progress and OIC Australia's ability to support it had been heavily affected by the global COVID-19 pandemic. OIC Cambodia's reporting focussed on achievements made and next steps towards redundancy. It is a simple model of reporting, looking backwards and forwards, with the end goal in mind.

Despite the global pandemic, OIC Cambodia leadership had managed to take important steps towards redundancy. There had been agreements with key ministries, hospitals and universities. Speech therapy had been piloted in a government hospital. Demand for speech therapy had been stimulated across a number of sectors.

Looking forward, there were plans to set the curriculum for the first university course in speech therapy in Cambodia, have the profession formally recognised by the government and create a career pathway and workforce for speech therapy in Cambodia.

While there were some short-term metrics, the key factor to success was how these short-term achievements fed into the long-term goal of redundancy.

Current perspectives of success focus on a snapshot in time. Funders of redundant charities focus on the legacy that the organisation is leaving behind.

What gets measured gets managed. And how we view success changes absolutely everything.

Work out steps to a sustainable end point

Has the international donor community drilled its last well?" John Oldfield loves the silence that ensues when he lets this question hang in the air at conferences and meetings. John was the CEO of Water 2017, a year long advocacy initiative to integrate water security into US foreign policy. He was also the CEO of Global Water 2020, a three-year advocacy effort that ended in June 2021.

As someone who has led the demise of not one but two redundant charities, he is someone who I was itching to speak to.

Speaking on video call, he had just stepped inside his home, sweaty from mowing his lawn in Washington, DC. John was candid in summarising where things had gone wrong in the WASH sector, and how we could go about fixing it.

John's definition of the exit point — when Global Water 2020 would make itself redundant — was: "Triple the amount of funding coming in from the private and public sector in the United States going to the global WASH challenge."

John Oldfield

John and his team had certainly nailed the 'S' (for specific) in SMART. When a redundant charity has laser focus on their exit point and is as specific as Global Water 2020 was, they have every chance of making themselves redundant. Compare this to a traditional charity that states they are "working themselves out of a job".

It can be hard for charities to recognise that it might be time to close their doors, even in tough times. The Australian Institute of Company Directors (AICD) released a survey in 2021 on governance and performance amongst non-profits in Australia. On the back of a global pandemic, a truly unprecedented challenge for modern charities to collectively face, the majority of non-profits admitted that they were financially worse off than before. The most common priority of boards was to respond to the ever-changing operating environment they were working in. Despite these challenges, only 1% of non-profit leaders indicated that their charities would be winding up. Despite distress, charity boards were digging their heels in to ensure that their charities survived at all costs.

For John and his team, they avoided this dilemma by simply having fewer structures to dismantle. For starters, instead of setting up a non-profit, they used a fiscal sponsor model. John and his team were employees of this fiscal sponsor who received funding and took a percentage of it to take care of back-end administration. Perhaps one of the ways in which more charities can make themselves redundant is simply this: let's start with less in the first place.

In a world where identity around doing good is so strong, starting with less seems counterintuitive. University students talk about their life goal of starting a non-profit organisation. Blake Mycoskie, the founder of the controversial TOMS social enterprise, speaks of a "gravitational pull" to start something (Chan, 2019).

In 2006, Mycoskie founded TOMS after visiting Argentina and seeing the impact a pair of shoes could have on a child's life. TOMS' buy one give one model was simple. For every pair of shoes purchased in Australia or France, TOMS donated a pair to someone in a poor country (Kim, 2020). In 2019, TOMS declared that they had given away more than 95 million shoes in 82 countries (Chochrek, 2019).

The most obvious issue with TOMS' model is that the buy one give one model does not progress beyond "give a man a fish" mentality. It places the recipients of shoes in a lower position of power and assumes that wealthy, Western consumers understand better than them what is needed in their own lives. Simply put, no one asked if shoes were the one thing needed to improve their lives.

Then there's the economic issue of flooding a local market with free goods from overseas. Although the shoes that TOMS donated were not second hand, they may have had the same effect as well meaning but harmful second hand donations to poor countries.

In 2008, a study found that used-clothing imports significantly hurt apparel production in Africa. This one factor resulted in a 40% decline in production and a 50% decline in employment in the clothing manufacturing sector between 1981–2000 (Frazer, 2008). On a large scale, local clothing manufacturers simply cannot compete with free imported goods.

Mycoskie has previously said that he felt so strongly about people going without shoes that he would dedicate his whole life to this problem. While admirable, there's an obvious issue with this attitude, as noted by a local entrepreneur in the documentary *Poverty Inc.*, "He's going to supply shoes for people for the rest of his life [which] is implying that he would want people to stay without shoes for their life" (Miller, 2014).

When we make it our life mission to help those in suffering, and our worth revolves around this service, our ego demands that there are people remaining who need our help. Paradoxically, it means people need to remain in suffering.

Contrast this to my conversation with John Oldfield. It's clear that he's more interested in what solution is needed than to his attachment to the solution.

There's no doubt that Mycoskie's single-mindedness has paid off. In 2014, Bain Capital, an investment company, acquired a 50% stake in TOMS, valuing the company at $625 million, with Mycoskie owning the remaining 50% (Roumeliotis, 2019).

However, in 2019, due to plummeting sales and increasing debt, Bain took control of the company and ousted Mycoskie from leadership (Hessekiel, 2021). TOMS pulled the buy one give one model in 2021, replacing the scheme with a much more traditional impact program — donating money to partner charities in poor countries (Holman and Sutherlin, 2021).

"'What the sector needs is an advocacy organisation [with] no business model, no financial model, no perceived or actual conflicts of interest, no competitive stance to any other organisation in the space,' John said."

The contrast between Mycoskie and John Oldfield's use of language could not be more stark. The former is the protagonist at the centre of the story. The latter wants to become less and less relevant.

"What the sector needs is an advocacy organisation [with] no business model, no financial model, no perceived or actual conflicts of interest, no competitive stance to any other organisation in the space," John said.

By creating less, John was able to focus more on long-lasting impact than on self-perpetuation.

The results were stunning. With Global Water 2020, the team had expected it would take years to successfully advocate for the UN Secretary General to address the lack of WASH and healthcare facilities. They met with him in February of 2018. He issued a call to action in Washington one month later. In a sector renowned for delays and time wasting, this is an incredible result.

Despite these successes, John isn't quite satisfied that their model is completely effective yet. To aid further decentralised decision-making, John's dream is that advocacy money could go to people more aware of the realities of the problem.

Rather than advocacy money going to John, he wants to see funding go to his counterparts in "Every developing country, in every county in Kenya, in every state in Brazil and every province in China to professionalise advocacy for WASH and sanitation in those geographies".

That's where the redundant charities mindset takes you. To something bigger than yourself.

John demonstrates something that all redundant charity leaders seemed to have in spades. Humility accompanied with a healthy detachment from ego and identity. In refusing to wrap up his identity in his work, John is able to zoom out from the charity's needs and focus on producing something of value to the world.

Only do things that take us to the end

> *"It's not the daily increase but daily decrease.*
> *Hack away at the unessential."*
> *—Bruce Lee*

For Marianne Tellier, visiting Uganda for the first time as a 27-year-old in 2010 was a life changing experience. She noticed how disadvantaged women, in particular, were. Women seemed to bear the brunt of responsibility for making things work for their families, but often they didn't have the resources needed; they couldn't find the money to pay for school fees or to transport their children to hospitals.

Coming from Denmark, a penny drop moment occurred for Marianne while seeing poverty up close in Uganda. She noticed that women would often go to the markets and return home with just two eggs at one time. This seemed like a waste of time, until she realised that they lacked the capital to purchase more.

Marianne Tellier

Another financial stress occurred around menstruation. Every month, women were reliant on disposable products that were absolutely necessary in order to continue to work and look after their families. Marianne and her co-founder, Maria Hyttel, had used menstrual cups themselves. What if this one thing could make a big difference to Ugandan women?

One of the most common complaints in the non-profit sector is the limited budgets. Charities simply don't have the resources to solve a multitude of problems.

And yet, for charities to win over donors, they have to talk like they do. It's far more profitable for a charity to talk about everything under the sun that they can do.

Marianne realised that were she to focus on all the problems she saw, it would spread her resourcing too thin, and there would be no way she would make a difference in Uganda.

"For charities to win over donors, they have to talk like they do."

Every time an innovative solution that seems too good to be true appears in the developing world, disappointment ensues. Think of PlayPump for example. A fundraiser's dream, PlayPump is a piece of merry-go-round equipment for children in poor countries. As children spin the merry-go-round around, it would pump up water from below the ground, thus providing the village with drinking water. Sounds pretty great, right?

Less so when you learn that for it to generate enough water per village, children would need to play on it for some 27 hours a day (Chambers, 2009). The PlayPump was four times as costly as more effective water pumps and when breakdowns occurred, which was regularly, it was extremely difficult to fix. Behind PlayPump's failure was a lack of consultation with local people (Murphy, 2013).

If PlayPump is a fundraiser's dream, menstrual cups are probably down the other end of the spectrum. But this didn't deter Marianne who emphasises the importance of "finding something that really works for the populations you're trying to help", and "not just trying to squeeze something down on top of them that maybe works for you."

At the time, a friend of hers, who happened to be male, didn't see the value of menstrual cups. He urged her to join him in building up the Ugandan private health sector. It would have been easy for Marianne to take her eye off the ball and move into something more lucrative. But that's not what redundant charities do.

Having a redundant charity mindset means laser focus. It means deleting everything else that comes up and looks shiny.

For Marianne, this allows her and the team at Womena to focus on their end goal: have policymakers and the community be aware of the value of menstrual cups and include it in their budgets.

It is an incredibly ambitious goal to introduce something that isn't even well-known in Australia or Europe to a country like Uganda. Getting menstrual cups on the agenda there requires choosing only those activities that will take the Womena to their end point.

With OIC Cambodia, on one visit back to Australia, I met a very wealthy Australian entrepreneur with a significant connection to Cambodia. He asked to meet me because he was inspired by me giving up my comfortable life to help Cambodians, despite not having Cambodian heritage. After giving me a full 20 seconds to explain why speech therapy would have the most impact, he interrupted me mid-sentence.

It was clear he wanted me to do something else. He got out of his chair and beckoned a close colleague of his in the next room to join the conversation. This colleague then began to tell me about his project distributing hearing aids from China to Cambodian villages. His real purpose for meeting with me was not to listen and support OIC Cambodia, it was to use the charity as a distribution pathway for these hearing aids from China.

Putting aside the burning issues with efficacy — how would the hearing aids be repaired if they failed and who was saying that hearing aids were what the communities wanted — this was an obvious no for me. Even if it came with the promise of hundreds of thousands of dollars of funding, it was an obvious distraction for the charity, which had nothing to do with hearing aids on a day-to-day basis.

> *"Being committed to the redundant charity model means looking past quick wins."*

It may have been my Asian upbringing and deference to my elders, but in the presence of a very wealthy older man, I didn't have the guts to tell him no on the spot. I listened and I nodded. I thanked them both for their time. I mentioned that I would be in touch with next steps, and then never got back to them.

Saying no to this opportunity wasn't just about the fact that distributing hearing aids wasn't part of the plan for OIC Cambodia. It was also a fundamental misalignment in values, one that I could feel through discomfort in my own body when the idea was suggested.

Distributing hearing aids is a great example of well meaning charitable work. But it combines "give a person a fish" and "something is better than nothing" mentality concomitantly.

Being committed to the redundant charity model means looking past quick wins. It's about taking a path that avoids dopamine hits associated with short-term wins and social media posts. It requires a focus on the end goal and, above all, discipline.

Marianne has that kind of discipline, and it's going to get her to a point where Womena can make itself redundant. For her, redundancy is clearly success. Once this issue with menstrual cups is taken care of, she can focus on another solution, another region or another problem.

That's the discipline of a redundant charity.

Chapter 7

Executing an exit strategy

Create a space for emotions

When you combine the ego and sunk cost fallacy, seeing the demise of a charity is as much work emotionally as it is practically. It would be easy to think that, amongst the never-ending to-do list of tasks such as deregistration, closing bank accounts and handing over resources, there's simply no time for dealing with the emotional toll of this work.

But this would be denying what it means to be human. It would be denying the very features of working in charity that make it unique — the level of heart involved.

If a redundant charity is organised, it will have time bound exits and clear plans on the steps that need to occur before they can exit. Despite this, leadership needs to make sure there are check in points with team members to reassess progress along the way. This ensures everyone is on the same page and that there's space for the emotional journey of an exit.

There's a parallel here with Alcoholics Anonymous (AA), the fellowship for recovering alcoholics that has been shown to be more effective than therapy (Erickson, 2020). One of the keys to the success of AA is the well-known fact that there are 12 steps to recovery. It's clear from the beginning what participants are up against.

In this timeless book, *The 7 habits of highly effective people*, Stephen R Covey preaches the ability to focus on what's important when steps are clear. Having clear steps in the demise of an organisation prevents the possibility of mission drift.

"To live a more balanced existence, you have to recognize that not doing everything that comes along is okay. There's no need to overextend yourself. All it takes is realizing that it's alright to say no when necessary and then focus on your highest priorities" (Covey, 1989).

According to the team at Stewarding Loss, a consulting group from the UK that focus on organisations ending healthily, there are six distinct phases to ending an organisation's life:

1.   Pre-decision

2.   Taking a decision

3.   Committing to the ending

4.   Designing the ending

5.   Implementing the ending

6.   Beyond the ending to new beginnings

Knowing these steps in advance is one thing. But being able

to handle the emotional work that comes with implementing a charity's demise is another. One of the key tips to achieving this is to be hyper-organised (Stewarding Loss, 2022). Being organised means that there is space for the often unpredictable nature of emotions, because the more predictable and practical aspects are under control.

While teams within charities cannot predict the future, they can be as prepared as possible. Once a decision has been made about the ending of a project, performing a premortem can be a logical next step.

Unlike a post-mortem, where a medical professional analyses the causes of a person's death, a premortem gets ahead of the curve by predicting what might go wrong ahead of time. Developed by Gary Klein, a cognitive psychologist, the premortem's genius lies in its simplicity (Klein, 2007).

Teams simply gather for as little as 20 to 30 minutes to imagine a future where their best laid plans have failed. In the case of redundant charities, it might well be that their plans to hand work over to the government haven't come to fruition. Each person then spends a few minutes writing down why this project has failed.

The team is not only able to account for reasons for failure, but also start to plan out strategies to mitigate these reasons. As simple as this half-hour exercise is, the benefits are huge.

In 2010, a group of researchers trialled the premortem method with a group of university students to evaluate a failed flu epidemic strategy. They found that using the premortem method severely reduced the level of overconfidence that the team felt (Veinott et al., 2010).

Epictetus said, "You can't learn that which you think you

already know." A premortem helps teams aiming to make themselves redundant, by learning ahead of time what could possibly go wrong.

Performing a premortem can help with removing potential feelings of regret. It's also vital that teams spend time thinking about how they would prefer to feel when the job is done (Stewarding Loss, 2022). This is another tangible way in which redundant charities can work towards a defined ending.

After all, for time bound charities, it's entirely valid to say that the end has been achieved when a feeling of completion or satisfaction has been reached.

Taking this one step further, the CEO of a charity that was ending created a 'memorial book', a place for anyone — staff, volunteer, trustee or other stakeholder — to write down their memories, lessons learnt or feelings over the time that the organisation had been around (Stewarding Loss, 2022).

The memorial book remembered the organisation for what it was, generating a sense of pride. Much like a personal journal, it allowed people to process their emotions in a public space. It allowed people to validate what they were feeling.

Putting people in positions of power

The first thing that strikes me about Shawn Cheung is his incredible sense of humility and self-awareness. This might well be because Shawn is one of the few charity founders I've ever met with lived experience of poverty. Shawn's parents emigrated from Hong Kong to Canada, both with professional qualifications (engineer and social scientist) that were not recognised in their new home country.

Shawn Cheung

Shawn spent his time after school reading the job advertisements for his mother and cutting out coupons from magazines and newspapers to help the family save money. Shawn lived with his parents and his sister in a 75 square metre (475 square foot) home, with seven square metres (75 square foot) of that home taken up by a sump pump to avoid the house from sinking.

Shawn is disarmingly authentic. Although fundraising is a huge part of his role, he admits that it's not a strength of his, unless it's after 6pm and in a bar. In fact, funders of Raising the Village (RTV), the charity Shawn founded in 2012, have often begged him to let them pay for him to access further training in fundraising.

What Shawn potentially lacks in fundraising charm, he makes up for in spades when it comes to understanding his place in the big scheme of things and elevating others into positions of power.

RTV's entire model revolves around bringing communities out

of extreme poverty in a 24-month program that increases household incomes and develops surrounding areas. It's absolutely essential that, for this approach to work, Shawn and his team are able to determine what it is that people need, even if they are at the very bottom of existing power structures.

But RTV works in Uganda, a country that has seen its fair share of local government corruption, as well as colonial Western approaches to charity work for 50 to 60 years. It's a familiar pattern of Western charities coming in and telling local people what to do.

They would ask the question, "What do you want to achieve and what role can we play?" Often, the answer would be as simple as "gas money".

At the same time, the Western suspicion of the Ugandan government has resulted in charities avoiding engaging with the government. But Shawn has a refreshing spin on working with the government as "the owners" of the problem, the ones who will be around long term, and therefore the right people for RTV to engage with.

In contrast to traditional charities who come into meetings with government counterparts, guns ablaze with a solution that they are pushing, RTV asks the government what gaps they see. They would ask the question, "What do you want to achieve and what role can we play?" Often, the answer would be as simple as "gas money".

So how does Shawn and his team flip the script on Western top-down forms of development? Through using data.

RTV created a dashboard that uses GPS mapping, partner household-based activity and adoption information to guide decision-making at the field level. This is a tool that RTV has developed for their field officers and is soon to be rolled out with government counterparts.

That's the hard aspect of RTV's data-driven approach. The equally important soft aspect is trust. RTV puts people whose opinions matter in positions of power.

In comparison to the average charity that boasts about ridding the planet of polio or solving the education crisis in Africa, Shawn and his team are remarkably understated.

When asking him how they define success, Shawn says they ensure they are "contributing to the social fabric of our society, because we see ourselves as a single thread, not the entire blanket".

This mindset allows RTV to hold itself accountable to itself and the people they are helping in Uganda, not to donors. It's this remarkable level of self-awareness that makes RTV stand out as a redundant charity.

RTV is more than happy to honour this intention through graduating its local partners after 24 months, including working closely with them during six months of heavy implementation. The implementation that occurs is multifaceted. Firstly, there is almost always some open-ended intervention that is determined with local partners. This could be related to agriculture, livestock or WASH, for example.

In their approaches to foundations for funding, RTV will not necessarily specify in great detail what their intervention will be, instead referring to the methodology they'll use for the community to determine what is most valuable to them. This is a far cry from the majority of funding applications, which require specificity to the nth degree. Non-profits are supposed to know every detail in advance, down to the exact number of people who will benefit from their programs. In unstable environments, in an unstable time, this doesn't make sense.

RTV's second main feature is always working with the government in Uganda. This means that they are always bringing the government along for the ride, ensuring that their projects do not need to be funded forever.

Somehow, RTV manages to engage both government and Ugandan households at the same time — no mean feat when you consider that they are at opposite ends of the spectrum in terms of power.

So where does Shawn and RTV's ability to think differently about charity work come from? And, likewise, where does the intention to buck the trend of 50 to 60 years of colonial Western approaches to development come from?

"Our organisation is 99.5% BIPOC (Black, Indigenous, people of colour)," Shawn says bluntly. "When almost everyone is an immigrant or comes from Uganda, it changes the mindset that you bring to your work."

Shawn's point is remarkably similar to that of Prashan Paramanathan, the CEO and Founder of Chuffed, a fundraising platform based in Australia. Prashan made a similar observation in 2020, at a time when discussions around race were present in many people's minds. The world had just witnessed the brutal murder of George Floyd, and the associated Black Lives Matter movement had gained significant momentum.

Prashan pointed out the complete lack of cultural diversity

amongst boards of large philanthropic foundations in Australia. "Forty directors. Not a single person of colour ... It's time we had a conversation about what structural racism looks like in the non-profit sector — and the effect it's having in creating the problems that the sector is meant to be solving," Prashan posted on LinkedIn (Coggan, 2020).

Prashan went on to explain that a lack of cultural diversity means that funds are unequally distributed to BIPOC-led organisations.

This is evident in the inability of Black social entrepreneurs to raise investment capital. In 2019, a report from the United States stated that "The median funds raised by Black applicants (for their social enterprises) is $0, compared to $12,245 (A$17,433) [for] their white counterparts" (Echoing Green, 2019).

Prashan also stated that white-led solutions to poverty maintain the status quo rather than dismantle systems of privilege. Shawn agrees heavily with this point. Having people from culturally diverse backgrounds widens an organisation's understanding of power dynamics. These people need to be in positions of power to create structural change.

"I don't know how else to explain it," Shawn says. "I've worked in both, and you get a different type of leadership either way."

With his humble upbringing, Shawn himself seems to be in the right place to lead RTV. And under Shawn's leadership, RTV's cultural diversity contributes heavily to an understanding of power dynamics. When the right people are put in positions of power, beautiful things can happen.

Equally, when those who had power leave, the same result occurs.

Founders out

"I start with the premise that the function of leadership is to produce more leaders, not more followers."
—Ralph Nader

I want you to close your eyes and think about an imaginary founder of a children's charity. This person is likely to be charismatic, with a story that is as alluring, if not more alluring, than the work that the charity does.

Much like Blake Mycoskie, there's a drive to this person's story, an absolute imperative to help those less fortunate. This is both highly admirable and, yet, once you put more thought into it, highly questionable. As mentioned at the start of this book, there's an ego attachment to doing good that makes working in the charity sector different from other sectors.

In order for this founder to attract funds, there's a constant stream of photos on the charity's social media with the founder hugging children. People are highly polarised by this person. About a third of people think the charity is incredible and is improving the lives of thousands of children. Another third believe the founder is a narcissist. The final third are somewhere in the middle. They admit that while self-promotion is grating, the charity's work speaks for itself.

The organisation needs the personality of this founder to raise funds. That's human nature. We love a hero.

Similarly, the founder needs the charity. It's so ingrained in the founder's identity that it must be hard to know where the charity ends and the human starts.

It's hard to imagine this organisation existing without the

founder, who brings in donations. The staff literally rely on one person for their livelihoods.

As long as the charity relies on the founder, and vice versa, neither the charity nor the founder can make themselves redundant.

I've been involved with founding five charities and social enterprises. Yes, for someone highly critical of charities, I've started quite a few. As much as anyone else, I understand the attachment that comes with your organisation.

Much like children, charities that you start never seem to grow up. Even decades later, you're seemingly never really absolved of responsibility for them. You can never truly detach your ego from the charity.

"As long as the charity relies on the founder, and vice versa, neither the charity nor the founder can make themselves redundant."

I also believe that a founder's skillset suits a specific time in the genesis of an organisation. Much like this polarising founder, I can see within myself many of the same characteristics. There's a drive that is uncommon. There's a sense of righteousness, and a disbelief in the status quo. And there's a feeling that if you don't do this piece of work, no one else can do it.

It takes a lot of work and self-reflection for a founder to adapt over time to the maturity of the organisation. Very often the skills they began with aren't relevant over time. The key question for the founder is then: "will you adapt, or will you admit that you yourself are redundant?"

This is a dilemma that all founders — for-profit or non-profit — need to grapple with.

It's also worth noting that a foreign founder is often a founder on the basis of privilege. That's not to say that founders like myself don't have particular skills or characteristics that are admirable. It is to say that often what sets us apart from our local counterparts is privilege. If things were to go wrong with the organisation I founded, I would have just moved back to Australia, moved in with my parents and gotten another job. For someone living more on the line than me, that's not an option.

When I started OIC Cambodia in 2013, I had two non-negotiable principles in mind. Firstly, the organisation had to have an exit point and a strategy to get there. Secondly, the organisation had to be led by Cambodian people.

The latter principle was both moral and pragmatic. I don't believe it is the right of foreigners to solve problems for Cambodian people. And even though I had lived in Cambodia for five years and gotten to a decent level of spoken Cambodian language, ultimately I didn't understand how to navigate Cambodia as much as someone who had spent their whole life there.

Like most founders, my personality could easily be described as "strong", and a strong personality is a disaster for groupthink.

In *The invisible gorilla: and other ways our intuitions deceive us*, the authors describe an experiment where a group, with dominant and non-dominant personalities in it, decide an answer to a maths problem. Unsurprisingly, the group tended to follow the answers of the dominant personalities. What is surprising is *why* they followed them.

"For 94 percent of the problems, the group's final answer was the first answer anyone suggested, and people with dominant personalities just tend to speak first and most forcefully." (Chabris & Simons, 2010). It really is that simple. If your mind works quickly and you speak first, people are generally going to fall into line behind you.

It took this realisation for me to also realise that for OIC Cambodia to become redundant, I too, as the founder, had to make myself redundant. Regardless of how much I tried to fade into the background, I realised that in my position in Cambodia I would always be a dominant personality. Here's why:

1. I'm the founder

2. I'm extroverted

3. I'm male

4. I'm tall (by Cambodian standards)

Not one of these factors indicate that my opinion is worth more than anyone else's. But all of these factors make others listen to my opinion over others.

I made many mistakes with OIC Cambodia, too many for one book. But one thing that I am proud of was successfully handing over leadership of the organisation to a Cambodian woman, Chenda Net, in 2017. Supported by OIC Cambodia's team of Cambodian and international volunteers and staff, there is every chance of decisions being made that are relevant to the local context.

These days, when someone asks me for my advice on when the right time is for a founder to leave, I usually give the same stock

Chenda Net and Weh Yeoh

standard answer: "There is no one right time, but it's better to leave too early, than to leave too late."

A charity has to learn to walk without a founder, and making themselves redundant needs to be front and centre in their mind from the beginning.

Communicate and advocate

Almost every charity I have come across has a lot of heart. Especially those who rely heavily on volunteer labour. Passion and compassion are elements that charities have in spades.

And yet, particularly for smaller, privately funded charities, they are not seen as having the same level of professionalism that for-profit entities do. Fortunately, there are charities that belie this stereotype.

One of these is Water for People, an American international charity working in the WASH sector. They have a secret weapon to ensure they exit countries effectively: comprehensive spreadsheets.

There's something about water and sanitation that appeals to most people's level of empathy. Unlike other causes such as democratic participation or sexual health, everyone can picture a family drinking clean water from a newly installed tap, or a toilet being installed within a house.

Laura Burns

Kimberly Lemme

There's something clean (pardon the pun) about explaining the need for water and sanitation. It's so visual. Just as easily, however, when things go wrong, the reminders are just as visual. As a woman in Salina, Malawi, notes: "The broken hand pump is a constant reminder of our inability to escape from poverty" (Breslin, 2010).

As I meet Kimberly Lemme and Laura Burns, two of Water for People's senior people in learning and sustainability, two things strike me as obvious. The first is their natural flair for communication; Kimberly makes a point of telling me that their organisation isn't just full of engineers. The second is how detail-oriented they are.

"They have a secret weapon to ensure they exit countries effectively: comprehensive spreadsheets".

Like an engineer proudly explaining every detail of a bridge they designed, Kimberly and Laura show me a spreadsheet used to evaluate Water for People's progress towards redundancy in Rwanda. Immediately, I can't help but think about how different this is to how people perceive charities — unsystematic, based on personality and flair, but also amateurish. There's nothing amateurish about Water for People's deliberate approach.

Using a wide range of metrics from the quality of household water to public institutions, the team at Water for People is able to rate on a scale how adequate the level of water and sanitation is in a particular region. There's also a checklist called the Sustainable Service Checklist.

In contrast to the stereotype in the charity sector of talking about flying into a poor country and building a well, Kimberly and Laura speak about their work in terms of systems strengthening. It's a significant departure from the mindset of traditional charities.

"We can't just spit out the same numbers that lots of organisations do," laments Laura in reference to how they measure success, while also noting that their internal monitoring process is "a lot heavier than a lot of other organisations".

Kimberly recognises that this means their model won't be suitable for "large, highly restricted government grants most of the time", especially those that are "very timebound and very specific on the outputs". It comes as no surprise to learn that governments, often in control of the most resources, have not evolved quickly enough to support models promoted by redundant charities.

"It comes as no surprise to learn that governments, often in control of the most resources, have not evolved quickly enough to support models promoted by redundant charities".

According to the Australian Charities and Not-for-profit Commission, private donations and bequests account for about 38% of revenue in smaller charities (those that raise less than $250,000 a year). Funding from the government accounts for about 10% of revenue.

In charities on the other end of the scale (those that raise over $10 million a year), the proportions are flipped. Government accounts for about 48% of revenue, and private donations and bequests account for less than 8% of revenue (ACNC, 2021).

One way to interpret this is to conclude that governments, who fund in much greater amounts than private donations, wield significant influence through funding larger charities. In other words, governments play an enormous role in determining what success looks like in the sector.

Unfortunately, as far as looking at redundancy goes, that's not where we are seeing change. We're seeing it amongst smaller charities and smaller funding bodies.

Water for People communicates with their donors, often high net-worth individuals, to advocate for their approach. Their donors are highly flexible, are sick of the status quo and exhibit an often rare quality in donors — curiosity. It's this curiosity that Water for People capitalises on.

The work of a redundant charity cannot be simply to exercise its desire to exist in a silo. It needs to advocate for a better model to everyone, especially donors.

Part 3

Your Role in Redundant Charities

Chapter 8

Taking steps towards redundancy

Everyone: We need your voice

Confucius said: "To see what is right and not do it is want of courage."

It doesn't matter if you are the CEO of a major charity, a program worker in Ethiopia or just someone who occasionally donates to or volunteers with a non-profit. We all have a role to play in starting a conversation.

We can start that conversation with anyone. Whether it's the person on the street asking for money, the co-worker asking you to buy chocolates, or the friend asking you to volunteer on the weekend. We can ask them, "How is that charity or cause working to make themselves redundant?"

Very often, non-profits will trot out the line that they are actively working themselves out of a job. On the face of it, this sounds good, but it's much harder to answer the follow up question: "Great, by when?"

Armed with what you know about redundant charities, your job is simply to talk about the new way of doing things.

Charities: You can make this change

"For every thousand hacking at the leaves of evil,
there is one striking at the root."
—Thoreau

It can feel hard for charities to do things differently. It can feel like you're wedged in between donors and beneficiaries. But really, you're in the driver's seat.

You can change existing programs to focus on redundancy. When I teach university students the principles of redundant charities, I often run them through an exercise like this: They look up examples of symptom-addressing programs online and try to turn them into problem-solving ones.

For example, they look at programs to get girls into schools. The programs are run entirely by foreign non-profits and are dependent on foreign funding. The students then have to work out how the foreign charity can work with local partners to make themselves redundant. Using the principles outlined in this book, these students are able to change the approach of most charities to make them redundant.

Every time I run this exercise, students learn that there are very few charities that are truly focussed on redundancy. They see that perverse incentives don't exactly create an environment where redundancy is encouraged. But they also see that there is a way to set up programs with the end in mind. It is possible.

Once a ship is sailing in a certain direction, it can be hard to see how the course can be changed midway through the journey. And yet, I'm often contacted by someone to speak to an existing charity about how to make themselves redundant. There's already so much interest and motivation, now is the time for action.

In speaking to the public, it often feels like it's a race to the bottom for charities who will say or do anything to get donations. Imagine if charities used their knowledge and power to educate the public on a better model, rather than pandering to the public's needs. For charities and those that work within them, you absolutely can make this change.

Institutional donors: Use your power wisely

"The quieter you become the more you are able to hear."
—Rumi

There is a slow but obvious change afoot. This is evident in institutional donors around the world and through networks like the Australian International Development Network (AIDN), who are exploring better ways of using donor money. They are becoming aware of the power they hold and want to use their power wisely. The donors behind Water for People and John Oldfield's projects are good examples of this. They wanted to hold charities accountable while being flexible in their approach to charities.

Ultimately, flexibility empowers charities, and that has a flow-on effect on the way that charities treat their causes. If a donor is there to learn and to listen as much as they are to support financially, great things can happen.

For donors, they are constantly under pressure to get charities to show results, and to show them quickly. Funders often require six-month project updates from charities. They will hold them up against a set of predefined goals.

Embracing the redundant charities model requires patience from the donor and a willingness to walk alongside the charity. Donors should be celebrating the fact that they won't need to fund projects forever. With defined end points, redundant charities give donors the satisfaction that they too won't be needed forever.

If donors are to perform one vital function, it can be to regularly ask the question to charities: "So, tell me. How will you exit?"

'Beneficiaries': Believe it or not, you're in charge

The beneficiary is the main reason why the charity exists. The beneficiary could be a group of people who represent a concrete need, an ideal (such as justice) or a concern (such as the environment). It can be hard to believe that the beneficiary is actually the most important stakeholder in the entire charity equation. Ideally, the beneficiary should be in a position of power. After all, no charity or funder would exist if the beneficiary didn't.

It's also really important to recognise power dynamics within a group. For example, when foreign charities go to communities overseas, they often ask local people what their needs are. They might hold a town hall meeting, but they won't recognise that in asking village elders to gather their constituents, they haven't had any people with disability attend. Blankly asking a group what they need is a sure-fire way of ensuring that some people's voices are not heard.

It's important that beneficiaries hold charities to account in making themselves redundant. This ensures that charities cannot leave suddenly, without a clear plan to ensure that what they're leaving behind can stand on its own two feet.

Founders: You're great, but get out earlier

"There is one thing stronger than all the armies in the world, and that is an idea whose time has come."
—Victor Hugo

It's much easier to start an initiative with the end in mind, than it is to retrofit strategies to turn a traditional charity into a redundant charity. It's so much easier to get it right from the beginning while the charity is still an idea. For founders, recognise that you have a very specific skill set. This skill set isn't necessarily ideal for organisations as they move forward. And therefore, over time, you may become less and less relevant to the organisation you started.

In much the same way as redundant charities have to have a deadline, so too do founders. It's best to set a timeframe to leave, and hold true to it as much as possible. Think about the best person to take over from you, who has the skills that you lack.

But also realise that even the best laid plans don't often turn out the way you thought they would. In Cambodia, we hired and trained a replacement for me, the founder, for about a year before I was due to return to Australia. And then about a month or two before that end date, she realised that she wasn't ready to perform the role. Though, at the time, it was difficult to hear that news, I'm ever grateful for her level of self-awareness and humility. Fortunately, we convinced a then board member to come into the role and replace me as the leader of the organisation. Even the best laid plans don't often come to fruition.

For founders there is one very simple principle. Get out when it's too early, rather than when it's too late.

Conclusion

"To be truly radical we must make hope possible, rather
than despair convincing."
—Raymond Williams

We live in an era of unprecedented threats. There are seemingly endless causes within our consciousness. It would be easy to give up, to turn off, but that's not what humans are geared to do. We're a race of survivors.

When there are any number of choices available to us, the simple solution is to focus. Focus our energies on the things that matter. Ensure that our limited resources are deployed towards actions that make a difference. That's what a redundant charity is all about. It's about focus.

One of the difficult parts of writing this book has been deciding whether the word charity is appropriate to use. As simple as this sounds, there have been so many negative associations with the word charity. Charities are thought of as wasteful. As amateurish. And as self-serving.

People who work within charities try to ignore this or often get defensive when it is raised. As affronting as this reality is, it presents an opportunity. We can use this moment to redefine what a successful charity is.

Until we have consensus on what a successful charity is, we'll never agree on what a successful charity should do.

WaterSHED's Geoff Revell believes that most donors see charities like machines where you feed it inputs and it generates outputs. A donor wants to see X return for their Y input.

This logic makes complete sense in theory or in a controlled environment like, for example, a laboratory. But the unstable, unpredictable world we live in could not be further from that environment. The naivety of this approach limits the scope of what charities can do, and we are all worse off for it. When you see a charity as a machine, you see a linear relationship between inputs and outputs.

"A redundant charity is far more aspirational. The relationship between inputs and outputs is more exponential than linear."

A redundant charity is far more aspirational. The relationship between inputs and outputs is more exponential than linear. This is because redundant charities are vehicles for catalytic change.

Rather than only influencing the microenvironment around them, a redundant charity catalyses change and alters the entire system. It recognises that, in the big scheme of things, its access to resources is minute. And so, it recognises that the greatest change it can create is the impetus for even greater change.

In recognising the lack of menstrual supplies in Uganda, Marianne Tellier did not follow the path of TOMS' Blake Mycoskie, promising to hand out free menstrual cups to all. That's the traditional linear approach. You give me a resource, I'll give out another. Instead, she thought about how to open up the market to menstrual cups within the country and how to ensure the market sustained itself. That's the difference between working within the system and working to change the system.

What happens next?

Keep the conversation going by visiting redundantcharities.com, and take the pledge to end the cycle of dependence.

Acknowledgements:

This book has been the culmination of over a decade of thinking, discussing and implementing different ideas to make charities more effective. It would be simply impossible to list all of the people who have helped and supported me along the way. However, I am extremely grateful for the love, guidance and support that I have received in putting together this book, and the charities that I've been involved in who are truly working to make themselves redundant. Although it is my name on the cover of this book, and often it's my name on various awards, it goes without saying that this is truly a team effort. From the bottom of my heart, thank you to everyone who has been involved.

Specific to this book, I'm hugely indebted to Aaron Scott for being able to finesse ideas and words in a way that only he could. To Kelly Irving for supporting this idea and facilitating connections above and beyond. To Robert Andersson for his generosity and time. To Jo Muirhead for believing in me and her excitement that I was finally writing a book on this topic. To Shani Raja for his practical and moral support. To Kenneth Watkins and Richard Freudenstein for their generous advice and wisdom. To Maxine Hawker for agreeing to roll up her sleeves and help out where needed. To Claire Salter Parry for her kind love and support.

I'm extremely grateful for the high quality work of Lu Sexton,

Stephanie Preston, Tania Favazza and Luke Harris in editing and design.

Thank you to the entire team at OIC Cambodia and OIC Australia for believing in this book. And to the Umbo team for supporting me and giving me the space to get it done.

A huge thank you to the trailblazers working in the Redundant Charities who I interviewed, firstly for their generosity of time, but also for allowing me to chase them for more information while they lead their busy lives. Thank you to Eric Stowe, Marianne Tellier, Kimberley Lemme, Laura Burns, Shawn Cheung, John Oldfield, Solomon King, Geoff Revell, and Sovattha Neou.

Thank you to Amber McBride for your love and support, and your belief that I could get this done. And a huge thank you to my family for supporting me, especially to my parents for encouraging me to challenge the status quo and creating solutions that support people in need.

References

ACNC. (2021, May 17). *Australian Charities Report — 7th edition*. ACNC.

Agenda for Humanity. (2019). *Grand Bargain*. Agenda for Humanity.

Ahmed, N., Dabi, N., Lawson, M., Lowthers, M., Marriott, A., & Mugehera, L. (2022). *Inequality Kills: The unparalleled action needed to combat unprecedented inequality in the wake of COVID-19*. Oxfam Policy & Practice. https://policy-practice.oxfam.org/resources/inequality-kills-the-unparalleled-action-needed-to-combat-unprecedented-inequal-621341/

Australian Institute of Company Directors. (2021, November). *Not-for-Profit Governance and Performance Study 2021*. http://www.companydirectors.com.au/nfpstudy2021

Bah, V. (2016). *Will the sky fall when big NGOs move south?* OpenDemocracy. https://www.opendemocracy.net/en/5050/will-sky-fall-when-big-ngos-move-south/

Bariyo, N., & Orden, E. (2012). *"Kony" Screening Inflames Ugandans*. Wall Street Journal.

Boddy, N. (2020, July 23). *How to make the leap from corporate to not-for-profit*. AFR.

Bosten, M. (2021). *Sunk Cost Fallacy: Throwing good money after bad*. Neurofied.

Breslin, E. D. (2010, August). *Rethinking Hydrophilanthropy: Smart Money for Transformative Impact*. Journal of Contemporary Water Research & Education, 145(1), 65–73.

Byanyima, W. (2016). *Oxfam International signs historic deal to move to Nairobi, Kenya*. Oxfam India.

Chabris, C. F., & Simons, D. J. (2010). *The Invisible Gorilla: And Other Ways Our Intuitions Deceive Us*. Crown.

Chambers, A. (2009, November 24). *Africa's not-so-magic roundabout*. The Guardian. https://www.theguardian.com/commentisfree/2009/nov/24/africa-charity-water-pumps-roundabouts

Chan, N. (2019, September 12). *267: How TOMS Founder Blake Mycoskie Blazed a Trail for Social Entrepreneurs*. Foundr. https://foundr.com/articles/podcast/blake-mycoskie-toms-shoes

Charity Navigator. (2019). *Rating for Wounded Warrior Project*. Charity Navigator. https://www.charitynavigator.org/ein/202370934

Chochrek, E. (2019) *As Toms' Challenges Continue, Brand Reveals It Has Donated Almost 100M Pairs of Shoes*. Footwear News. https://footwearnews.com/2019/business/financial-news/toms-shoe-donations-impact-report-1202876080/

Cole, T. (2012). *The White-Savior Industrial Complex*. The Atlantic.

Cooperation Committee for Cambodia. (2014). *Survey of Salary and Benefits, 2014*. Cooperation Committee for Cambodia. https://www.ccc-cambodia.org/en/resources/ccc-publications-and-reports/publications/survey-of-salary-and-benefits-2014

Covey, S. R. (1989). *The 7 Habits of Highly Effective People*. Simon and Schuster.

Daniel, L. (2021). *A Conversation with Bryan Johnson*. Junto. https://medium.com/jvnto/a-conversation-with-bryan-johnson-f00cad6f19d1

Domashneva, H. (2013, December 3). *NGOs in Cambodia: It's Complicated*. The Diplomat. https://thediplomat.com/2013/12/ngos-in-cambodia-its-complicated/

Erickson, M. (2020, March 11). *Alcoholics Anonymous most effective path to alcohol abstinence*. Stanford Medicine. https://med.stanford.edu/news/

all-news/2020/03/alcoholics-anonymous-most-effective-path-to-alcohol-abstinence.html

Feasey, N., Wansbrough-Jones, M., Mabey, D. C. W., & Solomon, A. W. (2010). Neglected tropical diseases. *British Medical Bulletin, 93*(1), 179–200.

Feather, N. T. (1974). Explanations of poverty in Australian and American samples: The person, society, or fate? *Australian Journal of Psychology, 26*(3), 199–216.

Forsch, S. (2018). Moving to the Global South: An Analysis of the Relocation of International Ngo Secretariats. *St Antony's International Review, 13*(2), 159–186.

Frazer, G. (2008) Used-Clothing Donations and Apparel Production in Africa. *The Economic Journal,* 118 (532), 1764-1784.

Giridharadas, A. (2018). *Winners Take All: The Elite Charade of Changing the World.* Alfred A. Knopf.

Grant, L. (1992). *Acts of Charity: Furious Donors Blamed a Lax Board After a Funds Scandal Toppled the Lavish-Living Head of the United Way. Now Can the Blue-Chip Agency Regain the Public's Trust?* Los Angeles Times.

Hessekiel, D. (2021). *The Rise And Fall Of The Buy-One-Give-One Model At TOMS.* Forbes. https://www.forbes.com/sites/davidhessekiel/2021/04/28/the-rise-and-fall-of-the-buy-one-give-one-model-at-toms/

Hoagl, J. (1993). *Prepared for Non-Combat.* The Washington Post. https://www.washingtonpost.com/archive/opinions/1993/04/15/prepared-for-non-combat/36160125-2420-47ca-9a79-01b2016d7ee5/

Holman, J., & Sutherlin M. (2021) *What Ever Happened to Toms Shoes?* Bloomberg. https://www.bloomberg.com/news/articles/2021-04-06/toms-shoes-ends-one-to-one-giving-model-in-turnaround-plan/

Hotez, P. J., Fenwick, A., Savioli, L., & Molyneux, D. H. (2009). Rescuing the bottom billion through control of neglected tropical diseases. *Lancet, 373*(9674), 1570–1575.

IFRC. (2015). *World Disasters Report — Chapter 4.* IFRC campaigns.

Incite! Women of Color Against Violence (Ed.). (2017). *The Revolution Will Not Be Funded: Beyond the Non-Profit Industrial Complex.* Duke University Press.

Insurify. (2020). *Major Motor Mishaps: Car Models with the Most Accidents in 2020.*

Kakuba, C., Nzabona, A., Asiimwe, J. B., Tuyiragize, R., & Mushomi, J. (2021, May). Who accesses secondary schooling in Uganda; Was the universal secondary education policy ubiquitously effective? *International Journal of Educational Development, 83*(102370).

Kan, S., & Klasen, S. (2020). Evaluating universal primary education in Uganda: School fee abolition and educational outcomes. *Review of Development Economics, 25*(1), 116–147.

Kim, I.A. (2020) *How Toms went from a $625 million company to being taken over by its creditors.* Business Insider. https://www.businessinsider.com/rise-and-fall-of-toms-shoes-blake-mycoskie-bain-capital-2020-3#:~:text=Serial%20entrepreneur%20Blake%20Mycoskie%20started,from%20celebrities%20and%20social%20media.

Kimberley, L. (2021, October 9). *Email Correspondence.*

Klein, G. (2007). *Performing a Project Premortem.* Harvard Business Review. https://hbr.org/2007/09/performing-a-project-premortem

Leach, S. (2018). *Aid Exits and Locally-led Development.* CDA Collaborative. https://www.cdacollaborative.org/wp-content/uploads/2018/04/Aid-Exits-and-Locally-led-Development.pdf

Max, T. (2017). *What's the Average Book Length & How Long Should a Book Be?* Scribe Media. https://scribemedia.com/how-long-should-book-be/

McClinton, D. (2019). *Global attention span is narrowing and trends don't last as long, study reveals.* The Guardian. https://www.theguardian.com/society/2019/apr/16/ got-a-minute-global-attention-span-is-narrowing-study-reveals

McVeigh, K. (2021). *Plan International accused of abandoning children in Sri Lanka exit.* The Guardian.

Merritt, A. C., Effron, D. A., & Monin, B. (2010). Moral self-licensing: When being good frees us to be bad. *Social and Personality Psychology Compass, 4*(5), 344–357.

Metcalfe-Hough, V., Fenton, W., Saez, P., & Spencer, A. (2022). *The Grand Bargain in 2021: An independent review.* ODI.

Miller, M. M. (Director). (2014). *Poverty, Inc.* [Film]. https://www.povertyinc.org

Murphy, T. (2013, July 2). *How PlayPumps are an example of learning from failure.* Humanosphere. https://www.humanosphere.org/basics/2013/07/how-playpumps-are-an-example-of-learning-from-failure/

Oxfam America. (2014, August 6). *Oxfam 2020, Tomorrow's Oxfam Starting Today, Induction Pack for Staff and Volunteers.* https://issuu.com/oa-padare/docs/confederationinductionpacken26feb-1

Oxfam International. (2014). *Oxfam 2020: Tomorrow's Oxfam Starting Now.*

Payne, L., & Fitchett, J. R. (2010). Bringing neglected tropical diseases into the spotlight. *Trends in Parasitology, 26*(9), 421-423.

Perton, M. (2022). *UK drivers trust GPS more than their own eyes.* Yahoo News.

Piff, P. K., Stancato, D. M., Côté, S., Mendoza-Denton, R., & Keltner, D. (2012). Higher social class predicts increased unethical behavior. *Proc Natl Acad Sci USA, 109*(11), 4086-91.

Plan International. (2022). *How we are financed.* https://plan-international.org/accountability/finance/

Ponniah, K. (2014, December 19). *Oxfam urges NGOs to mull exit strategies*. Phnom Penh Post. https://www.phnompenhpost.com/national/oxfam-urges-ngos-mull-exit-strategies

Revell, G. (2021, September 16). *Exit Strategies*. Stanford Social Innovation Review. https://ssir.org/articles/entry/exit_strategies

Roumeliotis, G. (2019, December 27). *Exclusive: TOMS Shoes creditors to take over the company*. Reuters. https://www.reuters.com/article/us-tomsshoes-m-a-creditors-exclusive-idUSKBN1YV1PT

Sanders, S. (2014). *Organization Behind 'Kony 2012' Set To Close Its Doors In 2015*. NPR.

Shapiro, R. (2011, November 14). *United Way leader's fraud scandal marred charitable legacy*. The Washington Post.

Shiffman, J. (2008). Has donor prioritization of HIV/AIDS displaced aid for other health issues? *Health Policy Plan, 23*(2), 95–100.

Smith, J., & Taylor, E. M. (2013). MDGs and NTDs: Reshaping the Global Health Agenda. *PLoS Negl Trop Dis, 7*(12), e2529.

Stark, L., Rubenstein, B. L., Pak, K., & Kosal, S. (2017). National estimation of children in residential care institutions in Cambodia: a modelling study. *BMJ Open, 7*(e013888).

Stewarding Loss. (2022). *Sensing an ending: A toolkit for nonprofit leaders to help decide, design and deliver better organisational endings*. Stewarding Loss. https://docs.google.com/document/d/14hsQgSqdootJgpkzcQkDCvsHv9QJiIAlCD2vG7cvw58/edit?usp=sharing

Vaessen, A. (2017). *Grand Bargain: Participation (R)evolution?* CHS Alliance.

Veinott, B., Klein, G. A., & Wiggins, S. (2010). *Evaluating the Effectiveness of the PreMortem Technique on Plan Confidence*. Proceedings of ISCRAM, Seattle, WA.

Water for People. (2018, June 13). *Creating a checklist for nonprofit exit*. Medium. https://medium.com/@waterforpeople/creating-a-checklist-for-nonprofit-exit-62104594cf9f

WaterSHED. (2021, May 24). *WaterSHED closes after successfully helping over a million people*. Phnom Penh Post. https://www.phnompenhpost.com/national/watershed-closes-after-successfully-helping-over-million-people

Weir, K. (2014). *The lasting impact of neglect*. American Psychological Association.

Weymouth, L. (2019, December 20). *Regulator criticises Marie Stopes over £434000 CEO salary*. Charity Times.

WHO. (2018, February 19). *Millennium Development Goals (MDGs)*. World Health Organization (WHO).

Williams, K. C. (2018). *Helpdesk Report: K4D — INGOs Relocating to the Global South — World*. ReliefWeb. https://reliefweb.int/report/world/helpdesk-report-k4d-ingos-relocating-global-south

Wounded Warrior Project. (2021). *2020 Annual Report*. https://www.woundedwarriorproject.org/media/wvsjamax/fy20-annual-report.pdf

Yeoh, W., & Smith, R. (2021). Email correspondence.

www.ingramcontent.com/pod-product-compliance
Lightning Source LLC
Chambersburg PA
CBHW041258040426
42334CB00028BA/3074